Australia's FAVOURITE RECIPES

Cherished family recipes from
around the country

Edited by Leila McKinnon

plum. Pan Macmillan Australia

Contents

FOREWORD

My Scottish parents brought their six children to Australia in 1929. We were overjoyed at our church-hall welcome. There were long tables covered with snowy white tablecloths and laden with trifles, chocolate cakes, sponge cakes with luscious strawberries and cream, and some with the delicious yellow seedy topping which we soon learned was called passionfruit. We were in seventh heaven and decided Australia was the place to be, with friendly, hospitable people, good cooks who enjoyed seeing their food being so appreciated.

We have so many families arriving in Australia from all over the world, bringing their traditions and recipes for the foods they treasure from their homelands just like the Scottish Fultons did. And looking through this book we find the wonderful variety of dishes from other cultures that Australians have learned to love and enjoy. These days, when we eat out, we can choose between Italian, Greek, Mexican, Chinese, Spanish and many more. It has made Australian food one of the most varied and exciting in the world.

Having spent a lifetime cooking, and loving every minute of it, I am not surprised that my daughter Suzanne Gibbs is a brilliant Cordon Bleu cook, and that my two granddaughters Kate and Louise have taken to life in the kitchen, writing cookbooks. That's what a love of cooking and sharing does for a family.

We have all had enormous pleasure looking through this book. Many of the recipes we know and love, and there are also new ones we want to try, from soups to seafood, vegetables, meats, desserts and cakes – what a choice. And if you want a glimpse of the past you will enjoy many of the pages featuring nostalgic ephemera and recipe books, all in all a reflection on days gone by, but cased in a look of today. This is a book to treasure and keep.

The icing on the cake, so to speak, is that the author's royalties and a portion of the publisher's sales are going to a charity very close to my heart, Legacy, who helps the families of our troops – the men and women who fought wars and gave so much to make our country what it is today.

Margaret Fulton

INTRODUCTION

When I grew up, parmesan cheese was still a smelly powder that came in a cardboard tube, and going to an Italian restaurant was an exotic night out. My mum, Josephine, is English and her rice pudding was the best dish on offer in our house, luckily it is a winner. To this day it only takes a spoonful of sugary, milky, gooey rice to take me back 30 years to our formica dining table in our tiny kitchen. My dad, Mac, is from New Zealand and he has the sweetest tooth I've ever come across. He didn't cook often, but my brother Daniel and I loved his saucer sized chewy Anzac biscuits made with triple the amount of golden syrup you will find in any other Anzac recipe. You'll find both of these gems plus a few others from my family in *Australia's Favourite Recipes*.

I distinctly remember going to a friend's house once and discovering the existence of tacos. They were made with spices from the packet but what a revelation they were. I made sure to get invited over most taco nights. On my birthday when I was about 10 years old I asked if we could go to a Chinese restaurant, I think I mainly wanted to use a lazy Susan, but how lovely to taste sweet and sour for the first time.

Of course baking with Mum or Nanna is a rite of passage for any child, if you haven't licked pancake or cake mix off the beater or spatula you have a right to complain about a deprived childhood. But these days children who cook have gone past us like we're standing still. Seeing the things kids eat, bake, stir-fry, and barbecue now is astounding. We often romanticise the good old days but there is no doubt that our palates and our health are much better off now than they were when we were shaking stinky 'parmesan' powder on our mince and calling it Bolognese sauce.

We didn't talk or think about food then the way we do now. Australia has developed a powerful passion for food, and the variety and quality of fresh produce, breads, cheeses, herbs and spices here is as extraordinary as you'll find in any country in the world. Turkish bread, Greek yoghurt, Thai herbs, Lebanese dips and spices; multiculturalism and the wonderful work of Margaret Fulton have brought the best in the world to our neighbourhood markets and stores.

Visitors from overseas are blown away by the riches we have at our fingertips. I've met world-renowned chefs and critics who were blown away at the fresh squid and seafood in our fish and chip shops, the richness of our cheeses and creams, the quality and range of our coffee, and the extensive selection of fruit and vegetables, from bok choy to white nectarines and beyond.

You really have to look in the right specialist corners in countries such as the United States for their quality produce. It's all there, but most bread is so sugary it is practically cake, cheese is bland but melted on every single meal you order, and unless you are prepared to pay top dollar forget about fish. Most Australians don't even realise that our beautiful breakfasts and lunches in local cafes are of a higher quality than just about anywhere in the world.

As a reporter for the Nine Network I've not only had the good fortune to travel the world but also to be invited into the homes of thousands of Australians from Cooktown to Hobart, Cottesloe to Byron Bay. Families have not only shared their stories with me, from the tragic to the inspiring, they've also shared their culture and I've discovered the wonderful diversity of food being served up on tables across the nation. Out on drought stricken properties, in the mansions of the rich and famous, and within the much-loved suburban homes around Australia, families are celebrating, sharing and showing their love with food.

I love to unwind by making a meal for my family and friends. It doesn't have to be fancy, just tasty, nourishing and made with love.

I am not a chef, I am not even an outstanding cook, but when I'm at home I love to unwind by making a meal for my family and friends. It doesn't have to be fancy, just tasty, nourishing and made with love. Like a lot of Australians I have piles of cookbooks and food magazines but I have always coveted a very special set of recipes that are carefully guarded because they are rightly treasured. They are the recipes nearly every family holds close: Nonna's Ragù, Papou's Dolmathes, Aunty Tilda's Black Forest Cake.

These are the best recipes because they've been put to the test and loved, time after time. They wouldn't have been made year after year if they had been difficult to make, or filled with impossible ingredients. They are not the trend of the moment, or the demanding extravaganza you'd come up with to impress dinner party guests. They each have a story behind them and they are made with justifiable pride.

So I decided to do a nationwide call-out, to ask ordinary Aussie cooks far and wide to hand them over. And wow, did I get lucky. A magnificent array of recipes came my way, and with them some incredible stories of the family members who came up with the recipes or brought them to Australia from around the world.

I am so proud to have collected those recipes and that the final selection is now published here in *Australia's Favourite Recipes*. Choosing between so many special dishes was not easy. We wanted a wide selection that represented the diversity of cultures in Australia, as well as the traditional favourites. Unfortunately not every contribution made it into the final edit, there were simply too many, but I thank everyone who took part.

What we have ended up with though, is a book that will be the one you turn to when you want to make something for a special family occasion, an easy mid-week meal, or to bake a treat that your kids will always remember.

I'm also delighted that Legacy will benefit from this project. I chose Legacy because I can't think of anything more Australian than the promise it fulfils every day to look after the needs of families of our men and women killed or injured in the service of our country. It's the spirit of mateship and every single day Legacy provides caring practical help for the families left behind through pension advocacy, counselling, special housing, medical, and social support. They're also committed to nurturing children's education by contributing towards school fees, books, uniforms, and activities to aid their self-development and confidence.

Legacy currently supports more than 100,000 Australian widows, and nearly two-thousand children and disabled dependents. Legacy cares for all, from 104-year-old widows to six-month-old babies. Since the Iraq War in the 1990s there have been more than 50,000 veterans created and it's important that Legacy is there, ready to support veterans' families should they become incapacitated or pass away as a result of their service. I am honoured to include the recipes of three women closely associated with Legacy: Miriam Zariffa, Muriel McCabe and Pat Tompkins.

I hope, like me, you enjoy the recipes in this book. Thank you so much to everyone who shared the dishes so close to their hearts and the stories that came with them. In doing so, these recipes belong to the whole of Australia now, and it's such a pleasure to imagine them being passed down through many more generations and enjoyed by our kids, grandchildren, and descendants.

Leila McKinnon

STARTERS
& SNACKS

Egg 'n' Bacon Baked Potatoes

A friend gave me this recipe years ago. When I made the potatoes, my whole family liked them so much that we now make them regularly for dinner and for all sorts of other occasions.
— Deborah Wilson, Sale, Victoria

- Preheat the oven to 200°C.

- Scrub the potatoes and prick all over with a fork. Place directly on the oven rack or a wire rack, and bake for about 1¼ hours or until tender when pierced with a skewer. Remove from the oven and cool a little until you can handle them.

- Grill the bacon until crisp, then roughly chop.

- Halve each potato lengthways and scoop out the centres into a large bowl. Reserve the potato shells.

- Add the butter, milk and egg yolks to the bowl and mash until well combined. Add the bacon, cheese and parsley, season to taste and mix in.

- Whisk the eggwhites until stiff peaks form, then gently fold into the potato mixture. Pile the potato mixture into the potato shells and bake for 10–15 minutes until the tops are golden.

- Serve hot with rocket on the side.

SERVES 4

4 large potatoes, unpeeled

125 g streaky bacon, rind removed

15 g salted butter

3 tablespoons milk

2 eggs, separated

125 g cheddar, coarsely grated

3 tablespoons chopped flat-leaf parsley

sea salt and freshly ground black pepper

rocket, to serve

Creamy Avocado Dip

I wanted to come up with a delicious creamy dip to enjoy at home and to take to functions. This dip fits the bill; it's tasty, quick and perfect for anyone who's lactose-intolerant. When avocados are in season, this dip is always in my fridge. I like to serve it with raw vegetables to keep it healthy, or crackers. My trick to prevent the dip from turning brown is to save the stone and pop it back in the dip after you've made it. — Ronnie Sallon, Coffs Harbour, NSW

- Halve each avocado lengthways. Remove the stones and reserve. Remove the flesh and roughly mash in a bowl.

- Stir in the lemon juice and garlic, add the yoghurt if using, and season to taste.

- Transfer to a serving bowl and serve with the vegetables or crackers. If not using immediately, place an avocado stone in the dip, cover with plastic wrap and refrigerate until serving. Remove the stone before serving.

SERVES 4

2 ripe avocados

juice of ½ lemon

2 garlic cloves, crushed

1 tablespoon plain yoghurt (optional)

sea salt and freshly ground black pepper

assorted raw vegetables or crackers, to serve

Eggplant Fritters

This dish originates from southern Italy, where eggplant is a staple of the cuisine. The recipe is something of a family treasure and has been handed down to me through many Italian generations. — Silvana Cursio, Craigieburn, Victoria

- Preheat the oven to 120°C.

- Cook the eggplant in a large saucepan of boiling water until tender. Drain well and when cool enough to handle, remove the skin and discard.

- Place the flesh in a large bowl and finely mash.

- Add the breadcrumbs, cheese, eggs and garlic, season with salt and pepper and mix thoroughly. If the mixture is too wet to shape into patties, add more breadcrumbs. Working with damp hands, shape the mixture into 15–20 patties and flatten to about 1 cm thick.

- Heat 1 cm of oil in a large frying pan over medium–high heat, add the patties, in batches, and cook each side until golden. Remove with a slotted spoon and drain on paper towel. Keep warm in the oven while you cook the remaining fritters.

- Serve with a garden salad.

MAKES 15–20

4 eggplants, quartered

¾ cup fresh breadcrumbs, plus extra

¾ finely grated parmesan

2 eggs

2 garlic cloves, crushed

sea salt and freshly ground black pepper

olive oil, for shallow-frying

garden salad, to serve

THE
MENU
BOOK
&
REGISTER
OF·DISHES

PRACTICAL
GASTRONOMY

Garlic Prawns

Serve this Australian classic at a barbecue, party or lunch and you'll quickly have an empty platter. This is the easiest recipe, as long as you follow two simple rules: only choose the plumpest, juiciest local prawns, and don't overcook them. When they turn pink, they're seconds away from being ready, so take them off the stovetop as they will continue to cook in their own heat. A little bit of chilli adds just enough fire to the distinctive garlicky taste.
— Leila McKinnon

- Place the prawns in a large cast-iron frying pan. Add the garlic, chilli and oil and toss to coat the prawns well.

- Place the pan over high heat and cook for 1 minute, tossing occasionally, then reduce the heat to medium and continue cooking until the prawns turn pink and are just cooked through.

- Serve immediately in a warmed serving dish with the lemon wedges.

SERVES 4

20–24 raw king prawns, shelled with tails left on and deveined

8 garlic cloves, crushed

3 small red chillies, halved, seeded and finely chopped

3 tablespoons olive oil

lemon wedges, to serve

Goat's Cheese Tartlets

The tang of goat's cheese makes these tartlets hard to resist, and I find they're the perfect size for picnics, school or work lunches, party food, or for when you're asked to bring a plate.
— Brett Steel, Hobart, Tas.

- To make the pastry, sift the flour and salt together into a large bowl. Rub in the butter with a pastry cutter or your hands to produce a breadcrumb texture. Add enough water to bring the pastry just together and form into a disc. Wrap in plastic wrap and chill for 30 minutes.

- Lightly butter six 8 cm tartlet tins. Roll the pastry out on a lightly floured work surface to 3 mm thick. Cut out six rounds big enough to line the tartlet tins and use to line the tins, making sure to push the pastry into the edges. Trim off any excess pastry using a small knife. Prick the base of the pastry shells with a fork and chill in the refrigerator for 30 minutes.

- Preheat the oven to 180°C.

- Line the pastry shells with baking paper, fill with baking beans, pastry weights or uncooked rice. Bake for 15 minutes, then remove the weights and paper and bake for another 5 minutes or until the pastry is crisp and lightly coloured. Remove from the oven and set aside.

- To make the filling, place the eggs, cream and 2 tablespoons of the parsley in a large bowl, season with salt and pepper and whisk to combine.

- Pour the egg mixture into the baked pastry shells, crumble over the goat's cheese, and place ½ tablespoon of the caramelised onion in the centre of each tartlet.

- Bake for 15–20 minutes or until golden and set. Remove from the tins and serve immediately, scattered with the remaining parsley.

MAKES 6

4 eggs
½ cup pouring (single) cream
3 tablespoons finely chopped flat-leaf parsley
sea salt and freshly ground black pepper
100 g goat's cheese
3 tablespoons caramelised onions

Pastry
2 cups plain flour, plus extra, for dusting
pinch of table salt
150 g cold unsalted butter, diced
¼–⅓ cup iced water

Soups

Minestrone

This is my husband's absolute favourite soup, and in winter we have it once a week. It does take some preparation in terms of shopping and chopping, but if you make a large amount, it lasts for days – and my husband swears it tastes better the older it gets. For me the appeal is all about the garnish of pesto and grated cheese. Sometimes I leave the pasta and beans out and simply add them on the second or third serving to refresh the soup. It's healthy and hearty enough to be a meal on its own. — Leila McKinnon

- If using dried beans, soak them in cold water overnight. Drain and rinse in cold water.

- Melt the butter in a large saucepan or casserole dish over low heat, add the onion, garlic, pancetta, sage and parsley and cook for 10 minutes or until the onion is soft and translucent.

- Add the celery, carrot and potato and cook for 8 minutes.

- Add the tomato purée, tomatoes, soaked (or canned) beans, basil and stock and season to taste with pepper. Increase the heat and bring to the boil, then cover, reduce the heat to a simmer and cook for 2 hours.

- Break up the potatoes with a wooden spoon and adjust the seasoning if necessary.

- Add the asparagus, green beans, cabbage and pasta, bring back to a simmer and cook for about 8 minutes or until the pasta is al dente.

- Ladle the soup into bowls, top with a spoonful of pesto and scatter over parmesan.

SERVES 6

1 cup dried beans (borlotti, kidney or pinto), or 400 g can beans, drained and rinsed

50 g salted butter

1 large onion, finely chopped

3 garlic cloves, crushed

150 g pancetta, diced

4 sage leaves

1 tablespoon finely chopped flat-leaf parsley

2 celery stalks, finely sliced

2 carrots, diced

4 potatoes, diced

1 tablespoon tomato purée

400 g can chopped tomatoes

8 basil leaves

3 litres vegetable or chicken stock

sea salt and freshly ground black pepper

8 asparagus spears, chopped

120 g green beans, trimmed and sliced

¼ cabbage, shredded

150 g tubettini or other small pasta

pesto and grated parmesan, to serve

Cream of Pumpkin Soup

This is a firm family favourite and one I learned to cook when a girlfriend and I enrolled in a cooking class in the 1970s. I don't believe there is another pumpkin soup recipe quite like this one or that tastes better. — Dell Maw, Marsden, Qld

- Melt the butter in a large saucepan over medium–low heat, add the onion and cook until golden.

- Add the pumpkin, potato, stock and milk, bring to the boil, then reduce the heat to a simmer and cook for 30 minutes.

- Blend in a food processor until completely smooth – you may have to do this in a couple of batches.

- Return the soup to the pan over medium heat. Stir in the Angostura Bitters and cream, season to taste and gently reheat.

- Serve immediately, drizzled with the extra cream and garnished with chives, or refrigerate and serve chilled. Enjoy with crusty bread.

SERVES 6–8

30 g salted butter

2 onions, roughly chopped

500–750 g pumpkin, peeled, seeded and diced

2 small potatoes, diced

600 ml chicken stock

1 cup (250 ml) milk

1 teaspoon Angostura Bitters

300 ml pouring (single) cream, plus extra, to garnish

sea salt and freshly ground black pepper

finely snipped chives, to garnish

crusty bread, to serve

THE AUSTRALIAN TOWN AND COUNTRY JOURNAL

Circulation three times that of any other weekly newspaper in Australasia.

VOL. XXXVII.—NO. 941.]   SYDNEY, SATURDAY, JANUARY 21, 1888.   [PRICE {Single Copy, Sixpence. 25s. per annum in advance.

Alterations for advertisements for the first two and the last two pages should be received at this office not later than Friday.

Shipping.

ORIENT LINE OF ROYAL MAIL STEAMERS.

The following Royal Mail Steamships belonging to the ORIENT and PACIFIC COMPANIES will leave SYDNEY at 1 p.m. on the undermentioned dates for PLYMOUTH and LONDON, via Melbourne, Adelaide, the Suez Canal, calling at Naples and Gibraltar:—

ORIZABA	6184 tons	G. N. Conlab	Jan. 31
LUSITANIA	3825	A. Tillett	Feb. 14
LIGURIA	4666	G. F. Dixon	Feb. 28
AUSTRAL	5588	J. F. Ruthven	March 13
IBERIA	4702	J. W. Shannon	March 27
CUZCO	6116	Charlton	April 10
CUZCO	3945	J. H. F. Nixon	April 24

and fortnightly thereafter.

SALOON PASSENGERS allowed to break their journey.
ENTIRE CABINS reserved on most liberal terms.
Passage Money—Saloon, £55, £60 and £70
Second, £30 and £42
Third and Steerage, £15

EXCURSION RETURN TICKETS at REDUCED RATES.
REDUCTION ON THIRD-CLASS AND STEERAGE FARES FROM LONDON.—Facilities are now afforded for bringing out friends and relatives by the prepayment of Passage Money here at the following reduced rates :—

Open berths ... 11 guineas each adult
Four-berth cabin ... 16 guineas each adult
Two-berth cabin ... 18 guineas each adult

MANAGERS: F. GREEN and CO. and ANDERSON, ANDERSON and CO., Fenchurch-avenue, London, E.C. Full particulars on application to
G. S. YUILL,
General Manager in Australia.
29, Pitt-street.

NORDDEUTSCHER LLOYD.
IMPERIAL GERMAN MAIL.
Passengers are carried according to the requirements of the English Passenger Acts of 1855 and 1863.

MONTHLY LINE OF DIRECT STEAMERS
from
SYDNEY, MELBOURNE, and ADELAIDE,
to SOUTHAMPTON, ANTWERP, and BREMEN via COLOMBO, Aden, Suez, and Genoa,
taking passengers for London,
"connecting from PORT SAID by DIRECT MAIL and PASSENGER LINE to BRINDISI"—
will be dispatched as follows (if practicable):—

Steamer.	Commander.	Sydney noon.	Melb.	Ad'ld @ Semaphore.
NURNBERG	Engelbart	Feb. 2	Feb. 6	Feb. 8
HABSBURG	Von Gossel	Mar. 1	Mar. 5	Mar. 7

And thereafter every four weeks.
PASSAGE from SYDNEY to London and ANTWERP ... £13 0s to £65
BREMEN ... £13 10s to £57 10s.
Special Return Tickets to Europe.
Reduced Passage Rates to Colombo, China, and Japan.

Through Tickets in the First and Second Classes at reduced rates to the principal cities of Germany, via Brindisi or Genoa. Passengers and cargo booked through to New York, via Southampton.
Passage from United Kingdom and Europe can be paid here. For FREIGHT, PASSAGE, and all further particulars, apply to
FINCK and BETZ, Limited, Agents,
6, O'Connell-street.

DIRECT SERVICE TO ENGLAND.
PENINSULAR AND ORIENTAL STEAM NAVIGATION COMPANY.
The Company's Royal Mail Steamships will be dispatched from their Wharf, Circular Quay, as under, DIRECT to PLYMOUTH and LONDON, via Colombo, calling at Melbourne, Glenelg, and King George's Sound :—

Steamer.	Tons	Commanders.	Leave Sydney noon.	Mel- bourne 1 p.m.	Leave Glenelg
VALETTA	4919	J. Orman	Jan. 20	Jan. 26	Jan. 28
SHANNON	4189	J. S. Murray	Feb. 4	Feb. 9	Feb. 11
ROME	5601	W. Barratt	Feb. 18	Feb. 25	Feb. 25
VICTORIA	5900	G. F. Cates	Mar. 3	Mar. 8	Mar. 10
CHUSAN	4636	H. Wyatt	Mar. 17	Mar. 22	Mar. 24
PARRAMATTA	4771	H. G. Murray	Mar. 31	Apr. 5	April 7
CARTHAGE	5013	R. G. Stead	Apr. 14	Apr. 19	April 21
MASSILIA	4918	S. D. Shallard	Apr. 28	May 3	May 5

and thenceforth every alternate week.
Commencing with the Valetta. The steamers will also call at Aden and Brindisi, proceeding from the latter port to England.
Rates of passage money to Plymouth and London—First saloon, £60 to £70; second saloon, £30 to £37; third, £15. Brindisi, Venice, Trieste, or Marseilles—First saloon, £50 to £65; second saloon, £26 to £35. No Egyptian transit or Canal Hope.
SPECIAL RETURN TICKETS at REDUCED RATES.
Reserved Cabins on moderate terms.
Saloon Passengers may break the journey.
Passage-money can be paid here for passages from England. Liberal concessions made to families.
Passengers, cargo, and parcels are booked through to India, China, and Japan.
For all information, apply at the Company's Offices, 367, George-street.
J. WEIR, Manager.

MOLONG.—Mr. W. DALY has been appointed Agent for the Town and Country Journal and Evening News vice Mr. W. McKenzie.

COBAR.—Mr. S. E. COLLOU has been appointed Agent at that town for the sale of T. and C. Journal and E. News.

Shipping.

COMPAGNIE DES MESSAGERIES MARITIMES.
DIRECT STEAM COMMUNICATION from SYDNEY to MARSEILLES, via MELBOURNE, ADELAIDE, MAURITIUS, and SUEZ CANAL.
BOOKING PASSENGERS THROUGH TO LONDON OVERLAND via MARSEILLES.
Steamers under joint contract with the Government of France.

The service is carried on by powerful steamers of 4000 tons and 3000 effective h.p., built expressly for the Australian and New Caledonian line, which will be dispatched as follows :—

Steamer.	Commander.	Leave Sydney Noon.	Leave at Melbourne 1 p.m.
SALAZIE	Boulard	Jan. 21	Jan. 25
YAWRA	Popdenot	Feb. 18	Feb. 22
OCEANIEN	Didier	March 17	March 21

And thenceforth every 28 days.
Rates of passage money to Marseilles from £20 to £95, including table wines and the Suez Canal dues on passengers.
RETURN TICKETS issued at the following rates :—

	1st Class.	2nd Class.	3rd Class.
Available 9 months	£105	£68	£48
Available 12 months	£115	£56	£30

N.B.—Passengers' luggage conveyed free of cost from Marseilles to London.
For freight, passage, and further particulars, apply at the Company's Office, 13, Macquarie-place.
A. CONIL, Principal Agent.

UNION STEAM SHIP COMPANY OF NEW ZEALAND, Limited.
SAN FRANCISCO ROYAL MAIL SERVICE.

OVERLAND ROUTE to ENGLAND, via SAN FRANCISCO and NEW YORK, calling at AUCKLAND and HONOLULU.
Avoiding alike the heat of the Red Sea and cold of Cape Horn.
Under contract with the Postmasters-General of New South Wales and New Zealand, the steamers of the line are appointed to leave Sydney and Auckland for Honolulu and San Francisco EVERY FOUR WEEKS, sailing as under :—

Steamer.	Tn.	Commander.	Leave Sydney	Arrive at San Francisco.
ALAMEDA	3000	Morse	January 25	February 19
MARIPOSA	3000	Hayward	February 22	March 18

Each steamer carries duly qualified surgeons.
These steamers are fitted with electric light, and with a refrigerating chamber for ship's provisions, ensuring a plentiful supply of ice throughout the voyage.
Passengers are booked to San Francisco or through to European destinations, and have at San Francisco choice of the unrivalled Atlantic Steamship Lines of the Cunard, Inman, White Star, and other Companies.
All first-class passengers are allowed 250lb of baggage to San Francisco, and 250lb "Overland," free of charge.

THROUGH FARE TO LIVERPOOL.
FIRST-CLASS ... £63 to £66.

Time cards, railway maps, and guide books, showing all routes to any part of the United States, may be had on application.
For rates of passage and freight, and all other information, apply to
FRED W. JACKSON, Manager,
Margaret-street.

AUSTRALASIAN UNITED STEAM NAVIGATION COMPANY, LIMITED.
Swift Mail and Passenger Steamers are intended to sail as under for Melbourne and Fiji, from Circular Quay; Queensland, from No. 1 Jetty, Grafton Wharf:—
Noumea, Suva, Levuka (Fiji), Wednesday, fortnightly, at 5 p.m.
Melbourne (without changing in the bay), Tuesday, 5 p.m., Fridays, 5 p.m.
Brisbane and all Queensland ports, Tuesdays, Wednesdays, and Fridays, 5 p.m., Saturdays, 2 p.m.
Maryborough (without changing). Fridays, 5 p.m. (changing at Brisbane, Tuesday, 5 p.m.
Bundaberg and Gladstone (without changing). Wednesdays, 5 p.m.
Rockhampton (without changing), Wednesdays, Fridays, 5 p.m., and via Keppel Bay, Tuesdays, 5 p.m., Saturdays, 2 p.m.
Bowen, without changing, Tuesdays, 5 p.m.; Mackay, Townsville, Thcompsons, Cardwell, Mourilyan, Johnston River, Cairns, Port Douglas, and Cooktown, Tuesday, 5 p.m., and Saturdays, 2 p.m.
Thursday Island, Normanton (nearest point to Croydon Goldfields), and Burketown, Saturdays, fortnightly, 2 p.m.
Steerage passengers are provided with food and bedding. Saloon return tickets available six months. Tickets issued by ship's officers charged 5s extra.
BURNS, PHILP, and CO., Limited,
Agents,
10, Bridge-street.

Missing Friends.

ASHWORTH, WILLIAM.—Please send your address to C. DAVIS, Alma Cottage, Albion-street, Leichhardt, near Sydney.

BENNETTS—WILLIAM BENNETTS will feel grateful for any information respecting the whereabouts of his Brother, CHARLES BENNETTS, last heard of ten years ago at the Burra Burra mines. May be on some of the gold mines. Address, WM. BENNETTS, Black's Point, Reefton, New Zealand.

CATCHPOLE, THOMAS, butcher, late of Orange, write to G. GIBSON, Hereford Arms, Rose and Ivy streets, Darlington. Important.

CHODAT—If this meets the eye of FREDRICK CHODAT, or anyone knowing his whereabouts, please communicate with his brother, HENRI CHODAT, Post-office, Nymagee. News from home.

COLE—WILLIAM COLE, formerly of the 29th British Infantry. Important news for you concerning your wife and daughters, formerly of Hamilton, Canada. Kindly send address to Office of this Paper.

DUNN—If this should meet the eye of Mr. GEORGE CHARLES DUNN, or Mr. DICK TILLL, late of Bunery Station, please communicate with Mrs. GEORGE HOLLAND, care of John Buckley, Yanta Bulla, via Bourke.

DUNNE—should this meet the eye of WM. DUNN, late of Walgett and Nyngan. If she will write to F. NEVILLE, Solicitor, Bourke, N.S. Wales, she will hear something greatly to her advantage. Country papers please copy.

DOBNEY, Mrs., maiden name, MATILDA HOWITT, or her husband.—Should this meet the eye of above, a son of Mr. R. Taylor, of London, who is now in Queensland, wishes to find them. Mrs. Dobney was born in Lincolnshire, at Goxedly, near Corby, and is now about 30 years of age. Last heard of in North of Queensland. Information as to their whereabouts will be thankfully received. Apply, H. TAYLOR, care of Mr. S. E. Hill, photographer and stationer, Eidsvold Goldfield, via Bundaberg and Mount Perry, Queensland.

ELLIS—If this should meet the eye of ABRAHAM ELLIS, last heard of at Guigong, N.S.W., of Portland Dorset, or anyone knowing him, please communicate with his niece, Mrs. W. DAVIS, Yarraville, near Melbourne, maiden name SUSAN NAH ELLIS.

GRANT, JOHN WALLACE, please write to your father, JAMES GRANT, Huntriss Row, Scarbro', England, or F. CHAPPEL, Brisbane.

HUDSON—If this should meet the eye of CATHERINE HUDSON, or ELIZABETH, or EDWARD, late of Sydney, please write to your Brother, THOMAS HUDSON, care JOHN M'DONALD, Wardell-road, Richmond River.

HYLAND—ALFRED ALBERT and SYDNEY NIMROUD HYLAND would hear something to their advantage by communicating with their Father, A. N. HYLAND, Butcher, Simpson-road, Collingwood, Melbourne; or anyone knowing address of either would be remembered.

HARTE, MICHAEL, or WILLIAM MICHAEL HARTE, formerly Sergeant of Police, County Westmeath, Ireland, or WILLIAM HARTE, late at Tooral Station, N.S.W., last heard of at Seymour, N., are earnestly requested to write to their Sister MARGARET. Anyone knowing the present address of the above will greatly oblige by sending it to Mrs. M. JENKINS, Grange, Upper Murray, Victoria.

LINEGAR—WILLIAM and JOSEPH LINEGAR would feel indebted for any information respecting the whereabouts of their Father, WM. NATHANIEL LINEGAR, who has not been heard of since 1880. May be on some of the gold diggings. Address, J. F. LINEGAR, Police-office, Parramatta, N.S.W.

MACMULLEN, HENRY, native of Maclear River, late of Botany, write to MARTHA, Rockwood Vale-office.

MOTTON—EMMA MOTTON, formerly WARMAN, the wife of G. B. MOTTON, or anyone knowing her whereabouts, is requested to communicate with MARK MITCHELL, Solicitor, 52, Castlereagh-street, Sydney.

M'GRATH—If this should meet the eye of PATRICK M'GRATH, last heard of at Bengerstown, Lobbinstown, Stone, County Meath, Ireland, kindly communicate with his Brother, JAMES M'GRATH, Town and Country Journal Office.

METCALF—If this should meet the eye of WILLIAM METCALF, who sailed from Toxteth Park, Liverpool, England, in 1880, last heard of at Brindingamba Station, N.S.W., some years ago, his Brother JOHN would like to communicate with him. Address Mr. JOHN METCALF, Charley's Creek Silver Mine, via Bowen, Queensland.

MYERS, Mrs. JOSEPH—If this should meet the eye of Mrs. JOSEPH MYERS, once residing in Cumberland-street, Sydney, please write to JOHN ALBERT, Upper North Creek, Ballina, Richmond River. Leave your husband's address, as I have news of great importance for him.

MYERS, JOSEPH—If this meets the eye of JOSEPH MYERS, once seaman on board the Willing Lass, of Brisbane, Queensland, write to your Shipmate, JOHN ALBERT (nickname ANTONY), quartermaster on board the City of Brisbane (s.s.), when you were mate of the John Bull. Write to me at once; let me know where you are. I have something of great importance to tell you, last heard of at Electrical Beach. JOHN ALBERT, Upper North Creek, in care of A. O'CONNOR, Ballina, Richmond River.

ONSLOW, GEORGE—Would GEORGE ONSLOW who for years lived at the Lyttle River, kindly send his address to JOHN F.M. MITCHELL, Bringenbrong, Corryong, Victoria.

ROSS—If this should meet the eye of ALEXANDER ROSS, late of Freestone's Brickyard, Granville, please send address to JAMES LARKIN, Waverley, G.P.O., as he would like to hear from him.

ROGER—If this should meet the eye of JOHN ROGER, native of Aberdeen, Scotland, or anyone knowing his whereabouts, please communicate with his Brother, JAMES ROGER, Carpenter, Broken Hill, N.S.W.

WITHERS—If this should meet the eye of HENRY WITHERS, or MARY JANE WITHERS (brother and sister, or anyone knowing their whereabouts, kindly send address to JOHN PERRY, Elmore Station, via another Road. He left Kenswick Asylum in 1876, and Henry left some time after.

Missing Friends.

R. M'RILBY (late of the Detective Force), PRIVATE INQUIRY, MISSING FRIENDS, and GENERAL BUSINESS AGENCY OFFICE.
No. 42, ROYAL ARCADE, SYDNEY.
Absconders and wife deserters traced, and all kinds of confidential inquiries instituted. Evidence obtained in divorce, libel, fraud, and incendiary cases for the legal profession and others. Copies of wills, certificates of birth, marriage, or death obtained in any part of the world. Rents and debts collected.
From R. M'R.'s LONG EXPERIENCE in the Detective Force of New South Wales, Victoria, and New Zealand, and established agencies in all parts of the globe, he is in a position to conduct all inquiries with CAUTION, EXPEDITION, and STRICTEST SECRECY, and to faithfully and promptly attend to all business entrusted to his care.

ARTHUR CUBITT'S MISSING FRIENDS,
CONFIDENTIAL and GENERAL INQUIRY OFFICE, 52, THE ARCADE, KING-STREET, SYDNEY.
CERTIFICATES OBTAINED OF BIRTHS, DEATHS, and MARRIAGES.
PRIVATE INQUIRIES CONDUCTED DAILY by Mr. CUBITT. COPIES OF WILLS and other DEEDS PROCURED.
It is the only reliable Institution in the colony and HOLDS THROUGHOUT AUSTRALIA AN UNPARALLELED POSITION.
No similar office has been so long established, and the public should bear in mind that THIRTY-SEVEN YEARS' EXPERIENCE in every phase of inquiry must be a special recommendation, and give Mr. CUBITT a PREFERENCE OVER ALL OTHERS who, notwithstanding their specious announcements, are practically incompetent to give satisfaction.
AGENCIES THROUGHOUT THE AUSTRALIAN COLONIES, NEW ZEALAND, the UNITED KINGDOM, AMERICA and the CONTINENT OF EUROPE.

T. AND G. BARNES,
MURRUMBURRAH,
WHOLESALE and RETAIL STOREKEEPERS, WINE and SPIRIT MERCHANTS,
Have on SALE all kinds of AGRICULTURAL IMPLEMENTS and FITTINGS.
Agents for T. Robinson and Co., Melbourne Station Supplies, &c., &c. Purchasers of Wool, Tallow, Hides, and Sheepskins, or will make liberal advances on same, consigned to their agents.
Agents for the Town and Country Journal.

HOME ENTERTAINMENT.
MAGIC LANTERNS.
Amusement for Old and Young.
These celebrated sources of fun can be sent to any address in the colonies, carefully packed in wooden boxes, with instructions for use.
Lanterns, with 12 slides, about 60 views, complete, 4s 6d, 7s 6d, 10s 6d, 12s 6d, 15s 6d, 17s 6d, and 25s each; 17s 6d and 25s lanterns have nice chandeliers and two movable slides extra. Extra slides in stock. Genuine Waterbury Watches, 10s each. Note address
H. E. HUTCHINSON,
New York Novelty Co., 116, George-street, Haymarket.

D. MITCHELL and CO.,
WHOLESALE GROCERS,
WINE and SPIRIT MERCHANTS, and GENERAL IMPORTERS,
CLARENCE-STREET, SYDNEY.
OUR MONTHLY PRICE LIST, which is now in the 10th year of its publication, IS FORWARDED GRATIS the First of every Month, and may be relied upon for Lowest Market Quotations.
PEOPLE ABOUT TO START STOREKEEPING will find Our Price List A MOST USEFUL GUIDE, as Stores can be Sorted FROM 10s and UPWARDS.
OUR TEAS are especially Recommended for Strength and Flavor, and of Most Excellent Value.

Beetroot Soup

We seem to have claimed the beetroot as our own in Australia. Foreigners tend to think it's a weird ingredient to put in a burger or a sandwich, but it seems like a marriage made in heaven to me. This soup is a different way to serve beetroot. Once you've tried its earthy sweetness you'll be hooked. The gorgeous ruby colour makes the soup look sensational and its robust taste combines beautifully with the sour cream and chives. — Bernie Larkin, Mordialloc, Vic.

- Place the beetroot, stock and dill seeds in a saucepan, season to taste and bring to the boil.

- Reduce the heat to a simmer and cook for 40–50 minutes.

- Strain the soup through a fine-mesh sieve lined with muslin into a clean saucepan. Discard the solids.

- Gently reheat the soup. Ladle into bowls, garnish with chives and serve with crusty bread and sour cream on the side for guests to spoon into their soup.

SERVES 4

1 kg beetroot, peeled and coarsely grated

1.25 litres beef or vegetable stock

¼ teaspoon dill seeds

sea salt and freshly ground black pepper

snipped chives, to garnish

crusty bread and ⅓ cup sour cream, to serve

French Onion Soup

The first time I ever tried this soup was in France, where I guess they just call it onion soup. It was the perfect dish to enjoy on a cold Paris day. I'll never forget that first taste – the richness of the flavours combined with the lightness of the caramelised onions and broth. Now it's one of my family's winter staples. It somehow manages to be glamorous yet cheap, easy and comforting. — Joybelle McIntosh, Ringwood, Vic.

- Melt the butter in a large heavy-based saucepan over low heat, add the onion, sprinkle with the sugar and cook, stirring occasionally, until golden.

- Sprinkle in the flour, increase the heat to medium, and stir for 2 minutes.

- Add the stock, season to taste and bring to the boil, then cover, reduce the heat to a simmer and cook for 30 minutes.

- Preheat the oven to 230°C or the griller to hot.

- Ladle the soup into six 300–400 ml capacity ovenproof bowls or ramekins. Scatter the cheese over the slices of baguette and place one in each bowl of soup. Place the bowls in the oven or under the griller and cook until the cheese melts and is nicely golden. Cool for 5 minutes before serving.

SERVES 6

40 g salted butter

750 g onions, finely sliced

1 teaspoon white sugar

2 teaspoons plain flour

1.5 litres beef or vegetable stock

sea salt and freshly ground
  black pepper

½–¾ cup finely grated gruyere

6 thin slices baguette, toasted

Chicken Noodle Soup

No soup has more universal appeal than the good old chicken–noodle combination. Unfortunately the two-minute versions of this favourite have made it seem stale and packaged, but cooked properly it's healthy, hearty and fresh. My family recipe uses a whole chicken, and all the goodness and flavour in the bones permeates the broth. You can cheat and use a cooked chook, but you won't get the same rich taste. — Leila McKinnon

- To make the chicken stock, place the whole chicken, carrot, celery, onion, garlic, parsley, thyme, bay leaves and stock in a large stockpot. Season with pepper and add enough water to amply cover the chicken (at least 2 litres). Cover and bring to the boil over medium heat.

- Reduce the heat to a simmer and cook for $1\frac{1}{4}$ hours or until the chicken is tender. Skim the surface of scum and fat occasionally.

- Remove the chicken from the pot and set aside to cool slightly. Strain the stock through a fine-mesh sieve lined with muslin or a clean Chux, into a large bowl, discarding the solids.

- When the chicken is cool enough to handle, remove the skin and discard. Coarsely shred the meat from the bones and set aside. Discard the bones.

- Melt the butter in a large saucepan or casserole dish over medium–low heat, add the carrot, celery, onion and leek and cook until the vegetables have softened but are not coloured.

- Add the chicken meat and 1.5–2 litres of the strained stock to the pan, bring to the boil, then reduce the heat to a simmer and cook for about 20 minutes or until the vegetables are tender.

- When the vegetables are nearly cooked, add the corn kernels and noodles and cook until the noodles are al dente.

- Season to taste. Ladle into bowls and garnish with the parsley to serve.

SERVES 6–8

20 g salted butter

4 carrots, finely sliced

2 celery stalks, finely sliced

1 onion, finely sliced

4 leeks (white part only), finely sliced

kernels from 2 cobs sweetcorn

125 g thin egg or rice noodles

sea salt and freshly ground black pepper

roughly chopped flat-leaf parsley, to garnish

Chicken stock

1 x 1.5 kg chicken

2 carrots, roughly chopped

2 celery stalks, roughly chopped

1 onion, quartered

3 garlic cloves

1 handful roughly chopped flat-leaf parsley

4 thyme sprigs

1 bay leaf

freshly ground black pepper

VEGETABLES

Spinach and Ricotta Gnocchi with Butter and Sage Sauce

You won't find these little soft parcels anywhere in a shop. One day I was making gnocchi and I had some spinach and ricotta in the fridge so I decided to make stuffed gnocchi. They looked like golf balls on the plate – not very pleasing on the eye – but after a few more attempts, the gnocchi half-moons were born and have been a hit ever since. They can be made in advance and frozen; cook directly from the freezer. — Gina Ottaway, Flinders, NSW

- Place the potatoes in a large saucepan, cover with cold salted water, bring to the boil over high heat and cook until tender. Drain, then return to the pan, cover and set aside for 5 minutes. Peel the potatoes and, using a mouli or masher, mash until very smooth.

- Heat the oil in a frying pan over low heat, add the garlic and cook for 30 seconds or until sizzling. Add the spinach and cook for 1 minute or until wilted. Set aside to cool.

- Place the ricotta, parmesan, mozzarella and 2 eggs in a bowl and mix until well combined. Finely chop the spinach, add to the ricotta mixture and mix until combined. Season to taste.

- Sift the flour into a mound on a work surface and make a well in the centre. Add the table salt, mashed potato and remaining egg. Using your hands, bring the mixture together and knead until a soft dough forms, adding more flour if necessary. Divide the dough into four portions and roll out one portion on a lightly floured surface until 3 mm thick. Using an 8 cm round cutter, cut out rounds from the dough.

- Place 1 teaspoon of the filling onto one half of the rounds, fold over to enclose the filling and press the edges to seal. Place on a lined baking tray. Repeat with the remaining dough, re-rolling the dough scraps too.

- Cook the gnocchi, in batches, in a large saucepan of boiling salted water for 3–4 minutes or until they float to the surface. Remove with a slotted spoon, place in a serving dish, cover and keep warm.

- Melt the butter in a frying pan over medium heat and cook for 2 minutes or until bubbling. Add the sage and cook for 3 minutes or until crisp and the butter just starts to turn golden.

- Spoon the sauce over the gnocchi and season to taste. Serve with the salad and lemon wedges.

SERVES 6

3 large sebago potatoes (about 800 g), scrubbed but unpeeled

2 teaspoons olive oil

1 garlic clove, crushed

80 g baby spinach

300 g fresh ricotta

½ cup grated parmesan

½ cup grated mozzarella

3 eggs

sea salt and freshly ground black pepper

2½ cups plain flour, plus extra, for dusting

1½ teaspoons table salt

200 g salted butter

18 sage leaves

rocket and shaved parmesan salad and lemon wedges, to serve

Mexican Bean Quesadillas

Quesadillas are my family's guilty pleasure. We are absolutely hooked on the perfect trio of melted cheese, spicy tomato and avocado. This is a handy recipe to have for a quick hot lunch, and you can add any left-over roast chicken, lamb or beef for a more filling meal.
— Thai Poonasamy, Aspendale Gardens, Victoria

- To make the avocado mash, halve the avocado lengthways and remove the stone. Remove the flesh and roughly mash in a bowl. Stir in the lemon juice, coriander and chilli and season to taste. Set aside.

- Preheat the oven to 120°C.

- Combine the beans, chilli, coriander, onion, tomato and lime juice in a bowl.

- To assemble the quesadillas, lay a tortilla on a work surface, spread with a layer of the bean mixture, scatter over some of the cheese, and spoon over some of the avocado mash (or you can leave the avocado out at this stage and reserve for serving). It's best not to overfill the quesadilla or it will be difficult to flip when cooking. Top with another tortilla and set aside. Repeat with the remaining tortillas and filling.

- Heat a large frying pan over medium heat, place one quesadilla in the pan, making sure it remains flat, and cook for 4–5 minutes. Gently slide it out of the pan and, using two spatulas, carefully turn it over. Return it to the pan and cook for another 4–5 minutes or until golden and crisp around the edges. Remove and keep warm in the oven. Repeat with the remaining quesadillas.

- Cut into wedges and serve with the avocado mash if you didn't use it in the filling.

SERVES 4

400 g can red kidney beans, drained and rinsed

1 small red chilli, halved, seeded and diced

3 tablespoons chopped coriander leaves or flat-leaf parsley

½ red onion, finely diced

2 tomatoes, finely diced

1 tablespoon lime or lemon juice

8 large flour tortillas

¾ cup coarsely grated cheese

Avocado mash

1 avocado

2 tablespoons lemon juice

2 tablespoons chopped coriander leaves or flat-leaf parsley

1 small red chilli, halved, seeded and diced

sea salt and freshly ground black pepper

Mushroom Curry

When I immigrated to Australia more than 20 years ago I discovered mushrooms for the first time. I wanted to a create a curry recipe using them and after many trials I came up with this version. It's a contemporary recipe compared to what my parents and grandparents used to cook in Fiji, and although I've used the traditional spices I've given it an Aussie twist. This recipe reflects the multicultural influences in Australian cuisine. — Satya Prasad, Bossley Park, NSW

- Heat the oil in a large saucepan over medium heat, add the ginger, curry powder, mustard seeds, fenugreek seeds, curry leaves and chilli (if using) and cook, stirring constantly, for 1–2 minutes or until fragrant.

- Add the mushroom and salt and mix thoroughly. Cook, stirring occasionally, for 5 minutes or until the mushroom juices have evaporated. Add the boiling water and cook for 3 minutes.

- Add the tomato paste, fennel seeds (if using) and chopped coriander, cover and cook for 1 minute (or if using fresh tomatoes, cook until the tomato has softened and the sauce has thickened slightly).

- Garnish with the whole coriander leaves to serve.

SERVES 4 AS PART OF A SHARED MEAL

2 tablespoons vegetable oil

1 tablespoon finely grated ginger

½ tablespoon curry powder, or to taste

1 teaspoon mustard seeds

1 teaspoon fenugreek seeds

leaves from 1 curry sprig (optional)

1 long red chilli, finely chopped (optional)

500 g button mushrooms, cleaned, stalks trimmed, thickly sliced

2 teaspoons sea salt

½ cup (125 ml) boiling water

1 tablespoon tomato paste, or 2 medium tomatoes, finely chopped

1 teaspoon fennel seeds (optional)

1 tablespoon finely chopped coriander leaves, plus whole leaves, to garnish

KAN-DOO
Cookery Book

A Book of Every-Day Requirements,

comprising

a Number of Useful Recipes.

Issued by Eden Hills Parish Hall Committee, in aid of its Funds.

PRICE 6D.

REV. J. COLVILLE,
Rector,

Copies obtainable
CAWTHORNES LTD.,
Rundle Street.

FOR

Baby's Washing:
"BUNYIP
NAPTHA"
SOAP

Register Print, Adelaide.

Margy's Dal

I live on Chinamans Island in the middle of Lake Conjola – you can only get here by boat. There are eight houses on the island, but they are mostly holiday homes and I am the only permanent resident. It is a wonderful way of life and my house is ideally located to host barbies and parties. I have been making this dal for more than 30 years, and it it always the star attraction on these occasions, especially with vegetarians. — Margy Butler, Lake Conjola, NSW

- Place the lentils in a saucepan, cover with 4 cm of water and bring to the boil over medium heat, then reduce the heat to a simmer and cook until soft to the bite. Drain and set aside.

- Heat the oil in a large saucepan over medium–low heat, add the onion and cook until softened and translucent. Add the garlic and cook until softened.

- Add the curry powder, cumin and garam masala and cook, stirring constantly, until fragrant.

- Add the lentils, tomato sauce, sugar and lemon juice and simmer for 15–20 minutes. (As with a curry, the longer you cook the dal, the better it will taste as the flavours meld together.)

- Add more lemon juice if required. Serve with flatbread, yoghurt and coriander.

SERVES 4 AS PART OF A SHARED MEAL OR AS A DIP

375 g lentils, rinsed

2 tablespoons vegetable oil

2 large onions, diced

2 garlic cloves, crushed

1 tablespoon curry powder

1 tablespoon ground cumin

1 tablespoon garam masala

1 cup tomato sauce, or to taste

1 teaspoon white sugar

juice of 2 lemons, or to taste

toasted Indian or Lebanese flatbreads, yoghurt or sour cream, and chopped coriander leaves, to serve

Jewelled Freekeh Salad

This recipe is a mash-up of all the things I love about Middle Eastern food: the spiciness, the surprising sweetness and the freshness from herbs. This salad has become a family staple. The combination of the fresh ingredients with the heartiness of the lentils gives it both lightness and substance. It has a smoky-sweet flavour that complements the herbs. It's a very versatile salad. You can pair it with grilled meat or fish, but our preference is fried salty haloumi. — Steve Wide, Carlton North, Victoria

- Place the freekeh and 2½ cups of water in a saucepan, bring to the boil, then reduce the heat to a simmer and cook for 15 minutes or until the water has mostly evaporated and the freekeh is tender. Remove from the heat, cover and set aside for 5 minutes to steam. Transfer to a large bowl and allow to cool.

- Meanwhile, place the pine nuts and almonds in a small frying pan over medium–low heat and toast, tossing frequently, until lightly golden. Set aside.

- Bash the pomegranate all over with a wooden spoon to loosen the seeds, then cut in half and remove the seeds, discarding the white membrane. (You will only need the seeds from half of the pomegranate – reserve the other half for another use.) Set aside.

- When the freekeh has cooled, add the lentils, currants, most of the herbs and all of the lemon juice, season to taste and mix together.

- Divide among plates and top with the remaining herbs, the toasted nuts and the pomegranate seeds.

Note

- Freekeh is roasted green wheat. It's available from health food stores and gourmet food stores.

SERVES 4

1 cup freekeh (see Note)

3 tablespoons pine nuts

3 tablespoons slivered almonds

1 small pomegranate

400 g can lentils, drained and rinsed

⅓ cup currants

1 handful flat-leaf parsley, roughly chopped

1 handful mint leaves, roughly chopped

juice of ½ lemon

sea salt and freshly ground black pepper

Veggie Patties

It's sometimes hard to be a vegetarian at a barbecue – you have to make your way through the piles of sausages, juicy steaks and chicken kebabs till you find the bread rolls and a few meagre salads. This recipe is something that I came up with so I didn't always have to go hungry. The best thing about these veggie patties is that they are full of flavour thanks to the coriander and the curry paste. You can also play around with the vegetables you put in – pretty much anything goes, but this combination of beetroot and carrot, with lentils and chickpeas thrown in for texture, is definitely my favourite. Other great additions are pine nuts or ground coriander or cumin. — Kalu Smith, Thornbury, Victoria

- Combine the beetroot, carrot, shallot, coriander, lentils, chickpeas, pumpkin seeds and curry paste in a large bowl. Add the eggs and flour, season to taste and mix well (using your hands is best). The mixture will be relatively moist, but if it seems too sloppy, add some more flour until it becomes a bit firmer.

- Shape the mixture into 10 large patties and refrigerate for 1 hour. (You don't have to refrigerate, but it makes them a little bit easier to cook and less likely to fall apart.)

- Preheat a barbecue flatplate to medium and lightly brush with oil, or heat 1–2 tablespoons oil in a large frying pan over medium heat. Cook the patties for 5 minutes each side or until crisp, golden and heated through.

- Serve the patties with the pita breads, lettuce and sauce.

MAKES ABOUT 10 LARGE PATTIES

2 beetroot, peeled and grated

3 carrots, grated

5 red shallots, finely chopped (or you could use 1 onion instead)

1 bunch coriander, finely chopped (including stems if desired)

400 g can brown lentils, drained and rinsed

400 g can chickpeas, drained, rinsed and mashed in a food processor

½ cup pumpkin or sunflower seeds, toasted

2–3 tablespoons Thai red curry paste

2 eggs

¾ cup plain flour

sea salt and freshly ground black pepper

vegetable oil, for cooking

toasted pita breads, baby cos lettuce leaves and your favourite sauce, to serve

Seafood

Baked Salmon

I can't think of a better choice for a light summer meal than this easy baked salmon. The herbs complement the distinctive flavour of the fish beautifully and it's really up to you whether you prefer a zesty lemon squeeze or a creamy aioli on the side. We always enjoy this beautifully pink and green dish as part of our spread on Christmas Day, and while we always have plenty of ham leftover for Boxing Day, you've got to be quick when it comes to the salmon. — Leila McKinnon

- Preheat the oven to 180°C. Place the salmon on a baking tray.

- Finely grate the zest of the lemons into a small bowl, add the garlic and oil and season to taste. Rub the mixture all over the salmon. Cut the lemon into wedges and set aside for serving.

- Bake the salmon for 20–30 minutes or until just cooked, depending on the thickness of the fish.

- Meanwhile, soak the preserved lemon quarters in cold water for 10 minutes. Remove the pulp and discard, and finely slice the zest. Combine the preserved lemon zest with the herbs and set aside.

- Transfer the salmon to a serving platter, scatter over the herb mixture, drizzle with oil and serve with the lemon wedges and potato salad.

SERVES 6–8

1 side salmon (about 1.5 kg), skinned and pin-boned

2 lemons

4 garlic cloves, crushed

⅓ cup extra-virgin olive oil, plus extra, for drizzling

sea salt and freshly ground black pepper

2 preserved lemon quarters

1 handful flat-leaf parsley

1 handful marjoram leaves

1 handful coriander leaves

warm potato salad or simple green salad, to serve

Beer-battered Flathead

I always think the poor old flathead is probably the ugliest fish you'll ever see in your life, but it has the perfect texture and flavour. These days you now see flathead on restaurant menus everywhere, but there's no need for any fancy flavours with this great-tasting fish – a squeeze of lemon will do. — Ron Castorina, Manly, NSW

- To make the batter, sift the flour and salt into a bowl and stir in the melted butter and beaten egg. Gradually add the beer, stirring until the mixture is just smooth. Set aside in a warm place for 1 hour.

- Fill a deep-sided saucepan or wok one-third full of oil and heat to 180°C or until a cube of bread turns golden in 15 seconds.

- Beat the eggwhite until stiff peaks form and gently fold into the batter.

- Immediately dip the fish into the batter and deep-fry until golden all over. Remove with a slotted spoon and drain on paper towel.

- Season to taste and serve with chips.

SERVES 4

vegetable oil, for deep-frying
4 flathead fillets, skinned
sea salt and freshly ground
    black pepper
potato chips, to serve

Batter
½ cup plain flour
pinch of table salt
10 g salted butter, melted
1 egg, beaten
¾ cup (180 ml) beer
1 eggwhite

Salt and Pepper Calamari

Speed is of the essence here. Cook it quickly and gobble it down straight away. The eating quickly part is easy in our family as this is one of those appetisers that is never waved away. It's hard to avoid overcooking the squid, which turns to the texture of rubber in a nanosecond, but when you get it right it's like an impressive dish for a home cook.— Pauline Von Goes, Fitzroy North, Vic.

- To make the Sichuan pepper and salt mix, place the peppercorns and salt in a frying pan and toast over medium heat, stirring constantly, for 3 minutes or until the salt turns golden. Crush using a mortar and pestle until very fine. Store in an airtight jar.

- Combine the flour and 2 tablespoons of the Sichuan pepper and salt mix in a large bowl.

- Fill a deep-sided saucepan or wok one-third full of oil and heat to 180°C or until a cube of bread turns golden in 15 seconds.

- Dust the calamari with the flour mixture, shaking off the excess, and deep-fry, in batches, for 2–3 minutes or until crisp and golden. Remove with a slotted spoon and drain on paper towel.

- Serve immediately with lemon wedges.

SERVES 4

2 tablespoons Sichuan peppercorns

3 tablespoons sea salt

½ cup plain flour

500 g cleaned calamari hoods, scored and cut into 4 cm x 2 cm rectangles

vegetable oil, for deep-frying

lemon or lime wedges, to serve

New Australian
Cookery illustrated

Spaghetti Marinara

When friends or family come to stay from overseas the most common thing I hear is how lucky we are to have access to such incredibly fresh seafood at decent prices. I still think we don't make the most of that luxury, but my spaghetti marinara recipe is a good way to start setting that right. Most good seafood shops have a decent marinara mix, so all you have to do is make the sauce for an easy gourmet meal. — Leila McKinnon

- Heat half of the oil in a large saucepan over medium–low heat, add the garlic and cook for 1–2 minutes or until fragrant but not coloured.

- Add the tomato, oregano, basil, parsley, wine, salt and pepper and bring to the boil, then cover, reduce the heat to a simmer and cook for 40 minutes. If the sauce becomes too thick, add a little extra wine or water.

- Meanwhile, prepare the shellfish. Trim the mussels and scallops and shell and devein the prawns. Dry well. Heat the remaining oil in a frying pan over medium–high heat, add the shellfish and cook for 5 minutes or until just cooked and lightly coloured. Remove from the pan and drain on paper towel. Set aside.

- Cook the spaghetti in boiling salted water according to the packet directions until al dente. Drain and keep warm.

- Just before serving, add the shellfish and spaghetti to the sauce, combine well and heat through.

- Garnish with the whole basil leaves to serve.

SERVES 6

½ cup (125 ml) olive oil

4 garlic cloves, crushed

800 g can whole tomatoes, drained and roughly chopped

1 teaspoon chopped oregano leaves

1 teaspoon chopped basil leaves, plus whole leaves, to garnish

1 teaspoon chopped flat-leaf parsley

1 cup (250 ml) red wine

1 teaspoon sea salt

½ teaspoon freshly ground black pepper

1 kg shellfish (such as mussels, scallops and prawns)

500 g spaghetti

Thai Fish Cakes

Among our many blessings, Australia is incredibly fortunate in its quantity and quality of Thai food. Who would have thought the unique combination of lemongrass, shrimp paste, fish sauce and kaffir lime leaves would become so much a part of our national diet? When I was growing up a fish cake was canned tuna mixed with mashed potato and fried within an inch of its life – those days are long gone. — Anna Small, Brunswick, Vic.

- Preheat the oven to 120°C.

- Place the fish in a food processor and process until smooth.

- Transfer to a bowl, add the coriander, cornflour, fish sauce, curry paste, spring onion and egg and mix until well combined. Shape the mixture into 8 patties, about 1 cm thick.

- Heat the oil in a heavy-based frying pan over medium–high heat, add the fish cakes, in batches, and cook for 4–5 minutes each side or until golden. Remove with a slotted spoon and keep warm in the oven.

- Serve with lime halves, sweet chilli sauce and green beans stir-fried with red onion, garlic and chilli.

SERVES 4

500 g firm white fish fillets, roughly chopped

½ cup coriander leaves, finely chopped

3 tablespoons cornflour

2 tablespoons fish sauce

1 tablespoon Thai red curry paste

4 spring onions, finely sliced

1 egg

vegetable oil, for shallow-frying

lime halves, sweet chilli sauce and stir-fried green beans, to serve

MEAT & POULTRY

Lamb Souvlaki

Lamb skewers are a traditional Greek festive meal, enjoyed especially after the Easter period of fasting. My grandparents made the transition from living in Turkey (also known as Asia Minor) to Greece in the great population exchange in the 1900s. They brought with them a love of spices, tradition and the gift of sharing. — Frank Vella, Keilor East, Victoria

- Combine the lamb, paprika, garam masala, cinnamon, salt, pepper, oregano, thyme and oil in a bowl and mix well. Leave to marinate for 30 minutes.

- Preheat a barbecue grill plate or griller to medium–high.

- Thread the lamb and vegetables, alternating, onto metal or bamboo skewers (see Notes).

- Cook the skewers for 5 minutes each side for medium–rare or 10 minutes each side for well done, depending on the thickness of the meat.

- Squeeze some lemon juice over the lamb skewers and serve with pita bread, tzatziki and Greek salad.

Notes

- It's good to use a cut of lamb that is not too lean and has a little fat in it, so the meat will be moist and tender.

- If using bamboo skewers, soak them in cold water for 30 minutes before using to prevent them from burning.

MAKES 9–12 SKEWERS

500 g lamb shoulder or leg, cut into bite-sized cubes (see Notes)

½ teaspoon sweet paprika

½ teaspoon garam masala

¼ teaspoon ground cinnamon

2 teaspoons sea salt

½ teaspoon freshly ground black pepper

1 teaspoon oregano leaves

1 teaspoon thyme leaves

3 tablespoons olive oil

1 yellow or green capsicum, cut into 2 cm pieces

1 onion, cut into 2 cm pieces

18–24 cherry tomatoes

lemon wedges, pita bread, tzatziki and Greek salad, to serve

I Can't Believe I'm Enjoying Brussels Sprouts

Ingham, about an hour's drive North of Townsville, is rich in Italian history. For over a hundred years the Russo family have grown sugarcane on the same patch of land on the banks of the Herbert River, and they have always dined according to their Sicilian heritage. Cane cutting by hand has always been hard work. By night the workers demanded great food and plenty of it. So the good recipes survived. This one from Taormina, Sicily was handed down to a legend in Ingham, Sam Russo. When he married Keren, a Kiwi, she was on a sharp learning curve! Thankfully she passed the secret on to her daughter Natasha, who is the love of my life. It's so good, it turns my least favourite vegetable – the brussels sprout – into something irresistible! — Cameron Williams, Coogee, NSW

- Preheat the oven to 200°C.

- Place the brussels sprouts on a large baking tray, drizzle with the oil and lemon juice, sprinkle over the chilli flakes and season to taste. Roast for 30 minutes or until golden and tender. Try one to check. They should be soft with a toasted flavour. Set aside.

- Meanwhile, cook the pasta in boiling salted water according to the packet directions until al dente. Drain and keep warm.

- Grill the pancetta until crispy. Set aside.

- Heat the oil in a large saucepan over medium–low heat, add the onion and garlic and cook until soft and translucent. Add the crème fraîche and wine and stir to combine. The sauce should be thick and creamy.

- Add the pasta to the sauce and toss to coat well.

- Add the brussels sprouts and mix through.

- Crush the crisp pancetta in your hands and mix through the pasta. Serve immediately.

SERVES 3–4

500 g small brussels sprouts

2 tablespoons olive oil, plus extra, for drizzling

juice of ½ lemon

pinch of chilli flakes

sea salt and freshly ground black pepper

400 g long pasta

12 slices pancetta

2 brown onions, finely chopped

1 garlic clove, finely chopped

200 g crème fraîche

½ cup (125 ml) dry white wine (sip the other half while cooking)

Pancit (Filipino Chicken Noodles)

'Pancit' (pronounced pun-sit) is a national dish of the Philippines. I sometimes call it 'chicken noodle thingy' for my friends who don't know what I'm talking about when I call it pancit. Everyone makes it differently – some use chicken, while others use pork or beef. It's very popular at birthdays, as the Filipino people believe that noodles represent long life. It's also perfect to take on a picnic or a barbecue.

As a kid growing up in Australia, I didn't want to eat Mum's Filipino cooking – all I wanted was fish'n'chips or a meat pie! But when I was 21 years old, my beloved Mum passed away. I realised I had missed out on so much. I'd taken it for granted that she'd always be there and never learned how to cook from her. Cooking dishes such as this one make me feel closer to Mum, and it's like there's still a piece of her with us around the dinner table or at family gatherings. My husband tells me that my pancit, however, doesn't taste the way he remembers my mum's tasting. But that's okay, this one is my own. This is now the dish that everyone requests I make or bring along to a barbecue, and I quite happily do it – it's like bringing my mother into my life, sharing in the joy. — Julie Gibson, Albion Park, NSW

- Place the pancit and vermicelli in separate large heatproof bowls, cover with boiling water and set aside for 5–10 minutes to soften. Drain well and set aside. I prefer to cut the vermicelli noodles with kitchen scissors, so they don't get all tangled up with the pancit noodles later on, but some people don't like to cut noodles for superstitious reasons.

- Meanwhile, heat the oil in a wok or large frying pan over high heat, add the garlic and vegetables and stir-fry for 2 minutes.

- Add the chicken and stir it around a little bit to heat through.

- Reduce the heat to low or even take it off the heat completely – if you add the noodles when the wok is too hot, they'll stick to the base. Add the noodles, soy sauce and oyster sauce. Have a taste, and add more sauce if required. Give it a little bit of a stir.

- Serve hot or at room temperature with chillies on the side.

SERVES 10

230 g pancit canton (thin wheat-flour noodles)

100 g vermicelli noodles

1 tablespoon olive oil

2 tablespoons crushed garlic

2–3 cups chopped mixed vegetables (frozen or fresh, such as snow peas, green beans, carrots, broccoli, capsicum and baby sweetcorn)

1 roasted chicken, meat shredded

3 tablespoons soy sauce

3 tablespoons oyster sauce

finely sliced long red chillies, to serve

Middle-Eastern Bean Stew

This great winter dish has served my family well. It is the perfect tonic after a long day spent at school footy or netball training and a great way to feed a horde of hungry kids. We like to put homemade yoghurt over the top and eat it while a *M*A*S*H* rerun is playing on television.
— Leurice Gilbert, Guildford, NSW

- Melt the butter in a large saucepan over medium–low heat, add the onion and beef and cook until the meat is browned, breaking up any lumps with a wooden spoon.

- Add the tomatoes and stir well to combine.

- Add the green beans and cook, stirring occasionally, until they begin to soften.

- Add enough stock to cover the mixture by 3–5 cm. Stir in the tomato paste and season with salt, pepper and cinnamon to taste. Simmer for 1½ hours or until most of the liquid has been absorbed and there is a thick sauce.

- Serve with rice.

SERVES 4

100 g salted butter

2 onions, chopped

500 g beef topside, minced

400 g can chopped tomatoes

1 kg green beans, trimmed

vegetable or chicken stock, to cover

2 teaspoons tomato paste

sea salt and freshly ground black pepper

ground cinnamon, to taste

steamed rice, to serve

Fast Basil Beef

I really like the warmth and simplicity of this recipe and it's great comfort food for winter. My son has described himself as a meat-eating dinosaur, so a successful meal for me is red meat, fast and economical. This is one of the few dishes he eats without leaving anything on the plate. We grow our own basil and I think it makes the dish even more yummy.
— Miriam Zariffa, Riverstone, NSW

- Heat the oil in a large pressure cooker over medium–high heat, add the steak, in batches, and cook until browned all over. Remove from the cooker and set aside.

- Add the onion to the cooker and cook until soft and translucent, adding the garlic and basil when the onion is nearly softened.

- Return the beef to the cooker along with the tomatoes, wine, tomato paste, bay leaf and powdered stock and season to taste (see Note).

- Secure the pressure cooker lid and bring to high pressure over high heat, then reduce the heat to low and cook for 30 minutes. Release the pressure according to the manufacturer's instructions.

- Scatter with basil leaves and serve with creamy mashed potato.

Note

- Check the manufacturer's instructions for your pressure cooker and add a little bit of water if more liquid is necessary.

SERVES 6

1 tablespoon olive oil

1.2 kg chuck steak, diced

1 large onion, chopped

2 garlic cloves, crushed

½ cup chopped basil leaves, plus extra to garnish

400 g can chopped tomatos, semi-drained

½ cup (125 ml) red wine

1 tablespoon tomato paste

1 bay leaf

1 teaspoon powdered vegetable stock

sea salt and freshly ground black pepper

mashed potato, to serve

Lebanese Chicken with Lamb and Pine Nuts

I remember when growing up that a lot of my friends from school would enjoy coming to our place for dinner to share my mum's Lebanese food taught to her by her mother, Melia. Sita Melia's place was only a few streets away and every time we went to visit her, there was always food being prepared. It was like a restaraunt kitchen: vine leaves being wrapped, marrows being stuffed, tomatoes being chopped. It was culinary heaven.

   This dish came in very handy for my mother, who lovingly cooked for five boys, one girl and my dad. Being one of six kids, the strategy at dinner time was to go hard early so you could get seconds – this no doubt accounts for why I am such a fast eater today.
— Tim Gilbert, Maroubra, NSW

- Heat 50 g of the butter in a large stockpot over medium–high heat, add the chicken and cook until browned all over. Remove from the pot and set aside. Add half of the onion, garlic and mixed spice and 1 tablespoon salt to the pot and stir for 30 seconds. Return the chicken to the pot, cover completely with water, cover with a lid and bring to the boil. Reduce the heat and simmer until the chicken is tender, skimming the surface occasionally. Remove the chicken from the stock and, when cool enough to handle, coarsely shred the meat and any browned skin from the bones. Set the meat aside and keep warm. Discard the bones. Reserve 1 litre of the chicken stock for later.

- Meanwhile, melt 50 g of the butter in a large heavy-based saucepan over medium–high heat, add the lamb and cook until browned. Add the remaining onion, garlic and mixed spice, 2 teaspoons salt and ½ teaspoon pepper and cook until the onion is soft and is translucent. Remove the mixture from the pan and set aside.

- In the same pan, melt 25 g of the butter over medium heat, add the noodles, breaking them up roughly with your hands as you add them, and cook until lightly toasted. Add the rice and 2 teaspoons salt and cook, stirring occasionally, for 1 minute.

- Return the lamb mixture to the pan, add the reserved chicken stock, stir to combine, cover and cook over low heat for 20 minutes, then remove from the heat and leave, covered, for 20 minutes.

- Melt the remaining butter in a small frying pan over medium–low heat, add the pine nuts and cook, stirring constantly, until lightly golden. Remove from the pan and drain on paper towel.

- Spoon the rice mixture onto a serving plate, scatter over the chicken and pine nuts and garnish with the parsley.

SERVES 6

150 g salted butter or ghee

1 x 1.8–2 kg whole chicken

2 onions, diced

2 garlic cloves, crushed

2 tablespoons mixed spice

sea salt and freshly ground white pepper

500 g diced lamb shoulder

100 g vermicelli noodles

2 cups medium-grain rice

½ cup pine nuts

flat-leaf parsley leaves, to garnish

Lamb Racks with Rosemary

I was surprised to find when I lived in the United States that Americans rarely eat lamb. If only it was less popular here, where prices seem to have gone through the roof. But a lamb rack is hard to resist and if you add rosemary, lemon, pepper and honey, you've got a very special dish. I find it's a great one for a dinner party too, as you can leave the lamb to cook while you prepare the vegetables and serve the entrée. Just be sure not to overcook the meat – lamb should always be a little pink. — Michael Baxter, Gunnedah, NSW

- Preheat the oven to 180°C.

- Remove the fine membrane on the lamb using a sharp knife and lightly score the fat in a diamond pattern. Rub the oil and half of the lemon juice into the lamb and season with salt and pepper. Place the lamb, fat side up, in a roasting tray and add the garlic halves.

- Roast for 20 minutes. Combine the remaining lemon juice with the honey and brush over the lamb. Add the rosemary and return to the oven for another 15 minutes for medium–rare.

- Remove the lamb from the oven and rest for 10 minutes before serving.

SERVES 6

3 rib-loin roasts, each with 6 ribs (ask your butcher to cut for you)

1 tablespoon vegetable oil

2 tablespoons lemon juice

sea salt and freshly ground black pepper

1 garlic head, halved lengthways

2 rosemary sprigs

2 tablespoons honey

The Barossa COOKERY BOOK

SELECTED & CHOICE RECIPES

As-Good-as-It-Gets Lasagne

When you have a big dish of lasagne, you've got lunch and dinner sorted for days. Sometimes I make a big one for home and a smaller one for my lovely octogenarian neighbour Hazel, and her delight at receiving it makes all those dirty pots and pans worthwhile. — Leila McKinnon

- To make the ragù, heat the oil a heavy-based saucepan over medium heat, add the onion, celery and carrot and cook, stirring frequently, for 5–6 minutes or until softened. Add the garlic and cook for 1–2 minutes or until fragrant. Add the pancetta and veal and cook, stirring to break up the meat, until well browned.

- Add the tomato paste, reduce the heat to low and cook for 2–3 minutes.

- Add the wine, stock, tomato passata, rosemary and thyme, increase the heat and bring to the boil, then reduce the heat to a simmer and cook, stirring frequently, for 1 hour. Season to taste and add the parsley.

- Preheat the oven to 180°C.

- To make the cheese sauce, place the butter in a saucepan over medium heat and melt without browning. Add the flour, stir well to combine, reduce the heat to medium–low and cook, stirring frequently, for 2–3 minutes or until sandy in texture.

- Increase the heat, add 1 ladleful of hot milk and whisk in well. Continue to add the milk, 1 ladleful at a time, until it's all incorporated. Add the mustard, reduce the heat and cook, stirring frequently, for 3–4 minutes.

- Remove from the heat, add the cheese and stir well until melted. Season well to taste.

- Place half of the ragù in a 30 cm x 20 cm x 5 cm (3-litre capacity) baking dish. Top with a single layer of lasagne sheets, half of the cheese sauce, another layer of lasagne sheets, the remaining ragù, more lasagne sheets and a final layer of cheese sauce. Sprinkle with the cheese and bake for 30–40 minutes or until golden and the pasta is cooked.

SERVES 6

250 g instant lasagne sheets

50 g grated cheese (mix of parmesan and cheddar)

Ragù

2 tablespoons olive oil

1 onion, diced

2 celery stalks, diced

1 carrot, diced

1 garlic clove, crushed

125 g pancetta, diced

1 kg veal (silverside is excellent), coarsely ground

2 tablespoons tomato paste

½ cup (125 ml) white wine

1½ (375 ml) cups beef stock

1 cup tomato passata (puréed tomatoes)

1 rosemary sprig

2–3 thyme sprigs

sea salt and freshly ground black pepper

2 tablespoons chopped flat-leaf parsley

Cheese sauce

2 tablespoons salted butter

2 tablespoon plain flour

3 cups (750 ml) hot milk

1 teaspoon dijon mustard

150 g grated cheese (mix of parmesan and cheddar)

sea salt and freshly ground black pepper

All I Want for Christmas is Ham

This recipe is based on the one that my mother always made at Christmas. I loved the original, but I felt it needed a splash more booze and spice! If there is leftover ham, you can store it in a cotton pillow case in the fridge to make sandwiches for the next day, and the day after, and the day after. — Adam Heslop, Newcastle, NSW

- Preheat the oven to 180°C.

- With a sharp knife, remove the skin from the ham but leave the layer of fat intact and score a diamond pattern into the fat. At each junction of the scoring, insert a whole clove for decorative purposes. Place on a wire rack in a roasting tray and fill with 1 cm of water (so the glaze doesn't burn).

- Combine the marmalade, whisky, oil, mustard, honey and ground cloves in a microwave-proof bowl, season to taste and microwave for 1 minute. Remove and stir, then coat the ham using half of the mixture.

- Roast the ham for about 1 hour or until the fat is golden and caramelised, basting the ham every 20 minutes with about 2 tablespoons of the remaining marmalade mixture.

- Remove from the oven and rest for 10 minutes before carving. Enjoy hot or at room temperature.

SERVES 25–30 (OR 10–15 WITH LEFTOVERS FOR SANDWICHES)

1 x 5–6 kg easy-carve ham leg

25 whole cloves, to decorate

500 g marmalade

½ cup (125 ml) whisky

2 teaspoons vegetable oil

2 teaspoons dijon mustard

3 tablespoons honey

1 teaspoon ground cloves

sea salt and freshly ground black pepper

Beef and Hokkien Noodle Stir-fry

This is my classic midweek stand-by. It's quick and simple. The lean beef and colourful vegetables make it incredibly healthy, and even my son always asks for seconds.
— Vivian Pearson, Erina Fair, NSW

- Cook the noodles in boiling water according to the packet directions. Drain and set aside.

- Heat the oil in large non-stick frying pan or wok over medium–high heat, add all of the vegetables and the garlic and stir-fry for 2 minutes.

- Add the beef and half of the soy sauce and stir-fry until the beef is cooked.

- Add the noodles and remaining soy sauce. Toss to combine and until heated through.

- Garnish with the sesame seeds to serve.

SERVES 3

350 g hokkien noodles

1 tablespoon olive oil

1 large carrot, finely sliced

1 small head broccoli, cut into florets

½ onion, finely sliced

½ red capsicum, finely sliced

½ cup frozen or fresh corn kernels

3 garlic cloves, sliced

300 g beef fillet, cut into thin strips

2 tablespoons soy sauce

toasted sesame seeds, to garnish

Roast Pork Fillets with Spiced Apple Sauce

Cooking for the people I love is my favourite pastime. My dad really enjoys a good pork roast, so for Father's Day I created and served him this version in appreciation for all the love and support he's shown me throughout the years. It goes really well with a cold cider! Cheers, Dad.
— Clinton Knop, Bunbury South, WA

- Combine the peppercorns, salt, cumin, fennel and coriander and finely grind in a spice grinder or using a mortar and pestle.

- Make tiny incisions all over the pork, drizzle with the oil and roll in the spice mixture to coat well. Refrigerate for 1 hour or overnight.

- Preheat the oven to 160°C.

- To make the apple sauce, place the apple and onion in a roasting tray, drizzle with the oil and scatter over the fennel, star anise, bay leaf and garlic. Bake until the apple starts to soften and the onion is slightly caramelised. Before the apple gets a tough exterior, pour over half of the stock and half of the cider and bake until the apple is tender.

- Remove from the oven and empty the apple into a saucepan, discarding any charred onion pieces. Add the remaining stock and cider, bring to the boil, then reduce the heat to a simmer and cook for 10 minutes or until slightly thickened. Strain through a fine-mesh sieve into a clean saucepan, pushing most of the softened apple pieces and liquid through the sieve. Discard the solids. Add the sugar to the pan and a little stock or water if necessary, and blend with a hand-held stick blender until smooth. Stir in the cream. Gently reheat the sauce just before serving.

- Increase the oven temperature to 180°C. Heat some of the oil in a frying pan over medium–high heat, add the pork and cook, gently turning, until coloured all over. Transfer to a baking tray and bake for 30 minutes or until cooked through.

- Remove from the oven and rest, covered with foil, for 10 minutes. Thickly slice the pork. Spoon the sauce onto each place and arrange 4–5 slices of pork on top. Serve with the orange and fennel salad.

SERVES 4

1 tablespoon black peppercorns

1½ tablespoons sea salt

1 teaspoon cumin seeds

⅓ cup fennel seeds

1 tablespoon coriander seeds

2 pork tenderloins (fillets) (400–500 g each)

1 tablespoon olive oil, plus extra, for drizzling

orange and fennel salad, to serve

Spiced apple sauce

5 granny smith apples, peeled, cored and cut into wedges

1 onion, cut into wedges

2 tablespoons olive oil

1 teaspoon fennel seeds

4 star anise

1 bay leaf

1 garlic clove, crushed

1 cup (250 ml) salt-reduced chicken stock

1 cup (250 ml) apple cider

2 tablespoons soft brown sugar

2 tablespoons double (thick) cream

Fettuccine Carbonara

My father was Italian and I have great memories of the magnificent feasts we used to have at home and at my relatives'. He and his brothers and sisters came from Belluno in Northern Italy in the early 1950s. My Uncle Antonio used to make his own wine and I remember squashing grapes in barrels with my bare feet in his shed. Two doors down from Uncle Antonio's was Uncle Giuseppe's place, where we used to help him make salami and other sausages. My uncles were all avid gardeners, having come from a farming background in Italy, and they used to grow the most wonderful fruit and vegetables. We would spend days preserving fruit, bottling vegetables and making tomato sauce. My aunties were always in the kitchen cooking something and they encouraged me to watch what they did and to help out. Those days are long gone as they have passed away, but their spirit lives on in my heart and my cooking. This carbonara is one of my favourite dishes. It was something that my father used to make, although I have tweaked it to make it my own. — Liz Thompson, Sunbury, Victoria

- Combine the eggs, cream and parmesan in a bowl and season with pepper. Set aside.

- Place the bacon in a large non-stick frying pan over medium–low heat and cook until the fat begins to render. Add the garlic and cook until softened. Add the sherry and spring onion and cook until the sherry has evaporated. Remove the mixture from the pan and drain on paper towel. Set aside.

- Cook the fettuccine in boiling salted water according to the packet directions until al dente. Drain, rinse under cold water to stop the pasta cooking further and return to the pan to medium–low heat.

- Add the egg mixture to the fettuccine, stirring to combine and coat the pasta well. Add the bacon mixture and give it a good stir. Garnish with the parsley to serve.

SERVES 4–6

3 eggs

⅓ cup pouring (single) cream

⅓ cup grated parmesan

freshly ground black pepper

6 slices middle bacon, rind removed but 5 mm fat left on, finely sliced

3 garlic cloves, finely chopped

1 tablespoon dry sherry (optional)

6 spring onions (white and green part), chopped

500 g fettuccine

3 tablespoons roughly chopped flat-leaf parsley

Quiche Lorraine

A real homemade quiche Lorraine tastes so much better than the store-bought versions. Sometimes I like to make my own pastry, and it definitely makes a difference. However, there is plenty of good-quality frozen shortcrust available, which means all you have to do is make the filling. My kids love this for a quick light dinner or hot lunch.
— James Clough, Brighton, Vic.

SERVES 4–6

- Preheat the oven to 190°C.

- Roll out the pastry to 3 mm thick on a lightly floured work surface and use to line a 20 cm loose-bottomed tart tin, making sure to push the pastry into the edges. Trim off any excess pastry using a small knife. Prick the base with a fork, line with baking paper, and fill with baking beans, pastry weights or uncooked rice. Bake for 15 minutes, then remove the weights and paper and bake for another 5 minutes or until lightly coloured. Remove from the oven and set aside.

- Meanwhile, place the bacon in a non-stick frying pan over medium–low heat and cook until crisp and the fat begins to render. Remove with a slotted spoon, leaving the bacon fat in the pan, and drain on paper towel.

- Add the onion to the pan and cook until soft and translucent. Remove from the heat and cool.

- Spread the bacon and onion over the base of the pastry shell.

- Combine the eggs, cream and nutmeg in a bowl, season with salt and pepper and whisk until well combined but not frothy. Pour into the pastry shell, then scatter over the cheese.

- Bake for 30–35 minutes or until the quiche is set in the middle.

- Remove from the oven and cool in the tin for 5 minutes before removing. Enjoy hot or at room temperature with rocket salad.

125 g store-bought shortcrust pastry

plain flour, for dusting

4 slices bacon, rind removed, chopped into 2 cm pieces

1 large onion, finely chopped

3 eggs, lightly beaten

⅔ cup (160 ml) pouring (single) cream

pinch of ground nutmeg

sea salt and freshly ground black pepper

125 g gruyere or Swiss cheese, finely sliced

rocket salad, to serve

Quick-and-Easy Bolognese

As the name suggests, this is a simple everyday sauce. I often double the quantity and freeze it in portions. Dinner is never far away with a tub of bolognese nearby. I pull it out of the freezer and it becomes the base of other dishes, such as shepherd's pie, chilli con carne, taco mince or lasagne. — Barbara Cluness, Elwood, Vic.

- Heat the oil in a large saucepan over medium heat, add the onion and cook for 3–4 minutes or until soft and translucent. Add the garlic and cook for 1–2 minutes or until fragrant.

- Add the beef and cook, stirring with a wooden spoon to break up any lumps, until well browned. Add the tomato paste and cook, stirring frequently, for 1–2 minutes.

- Add the tomato passata, stock and herbs and bring to the boil, then reduce the heat to a simmer and cook, stirring frequently, for 10–15 minutes or until the sauce has thickened to your desired consistency. Season to taste.

- Serve on top of pasta with parmesan scattered over.

SERVES 4–6

2 tablespoons olive oil
   or vegetable oil

2 onions, diced

2 garlic cloves, crushed

1 kg lean minced beef

3 tablespoons tomato paste

1 cup tomato passata
   (puréed tomatoes)

1½ cups (375 ml) beef stock

2 tablespoons chopped herbs
   (basil, thyme or parsley)

sea salt and freshly ground
   black pepper

cooked pasta and grated
   parmesan, to serve

Desserts

Apple Crumble

The beauty of this apple crumble is that you can make it from pantry staples. Keep a can of pie apples and a packet of biscuits on hand and it means a quick weeknight treat is only a mixing bowl away. It is lovely with custard or cream, and the recipe can be easily halved or doubled. — Jean Mills, Kings Meadows, Tas

- Preheat the oven to 180°C.

- Combine the butter and sugar in a bowl, add the crushed biscuits and mix well.

- Layer the pie apples in the base of a 2 litre capacity pie dish or 6 individual heatproof bowls. Scatter over the sultanas and ground ginger and top with the biscuit mixture.

- Bake for 30 minutes or until the top is golden and the pie is hot.

- Serve with the cream poured over.

SERVES 6

125 g unsalted butter, melted and slightly cooled

½ cup loosely packed soft brown sugar

250 g packet Scotch Finger biscuits, crushed

800 g can pie apples

pinch of ground ginger

½ cup sultanas

pouring (single) cream or custard, to serve

Grandma Storey's Golden Syrup Dumplings

I have the rosiest memories of visiting my grandma every month when I was growing up. She lived in a tiny, wonky, wooden house in a small country town called Oakey, which was a few hours west of Brisbane. In summer she would make caramel tart for dessert, and in winter it was always these golden syrup dumplings. She would cook them on her old AGA stove and we would eat them with lots of vanilla ice-cream. I love the fluffiness of the dumplings, swimming in their rich caramel sauce (the more sauce, the better!). Whenever I make them I am always transported straight back to my grandma's kitchen. — Alison Winning, Milton, Qld

- Sift the flour and salt into a large bowl, then rub in the butter and make a well in the centre.

- Combine the syrup and milk in a jug and whisk with a fork. Gradually add to the well in the flour mixture, stirring gently with a wooden spoon until just combined. Be careful not to overmix. Set aside.

- To make the sauce, place all of the ingredients and 2 cups (500 ml) water in a large saucepan over medium heat and stir until the sugar has dissolved, then increase the heat to bring the sauce to a simmer (but don't boil or the sauce will darken before the dumplings are cooked).

- Take rounded teaspoons of the dumpling batter and gently lower them into the simmering sauce. Cover and gently simmer for 25 minutes.

- Serve the dumplings hot with some of the sauce and a scoop of ice-cream. (Leftovers make a great breakfast the next day.)

SERVES 4

1¼ cups self-raising flour

pinch of table salt

30 g unsalted butter, diced

⅓ cup golden syrup

⅓ cup milk

ice-cream, custard or double (thick) cream, to serve

Sauce

30 g unsalted butter

¾ cup lightly packed soft brown sugar

½ cup golden syrup

Impossible Pudding

This recipe belongs to my mum. It's Australian, it's quick and the kids love it! When my four sisters and I were growing up mum would make this as a treat, especially in the winter months. We would devour it as soon as it hit the table. Now my own two children do the same when I make it for them. — Cate Wilkinson, Mango Hill, Qld

- Preheat the oven to 170°C and grease a 1.5–2 litre capacity baking dish or 6 individual dishes.

- Cream the butter and sugar in a large bowl until light and fluffy. Beat in the eggs one at a time, beating well after each addition.

- Sift in the flour and baking powder and fold in gently along with the coconut.

- Add the milk and vanilla essence and gently stir to combine. Pour the mixture into the dish or dishes.

- Bake for 45 minutes or until the top is golden. As the pudding cooks it develops a crusty exterior with a pudding centre.

- Remove from the oven and serve immediately.

SERVES 6

115 g unsalted butter, softened

1 cup caster sugar

4 eggs

3 tablespoons plain flour

1 teaspoon baking powder

1 cup desiccated coconut (or ½ cup if you're not keen on it)

2 cups (500 ml) milk

1 teaspoon vanilla essence

Lemon Pavlova

I have been making this pav for more than 25 years. It's so easy to make – no fussing about, just beat it all together. It has a beautiful marshmallow centre and the lemon filling adds a nice twist. On the rare occasion when there is any left over, it keeps well in the fridge. I love to share good recipes and ideas, and have passed this one on to so many people over the years. Even though my daughter has the recipe, she still asks me to make it for her. — Jen Brittain, Cobden, Victoria

- Preheat the oven to 200°C. Trace trace six 8 cm diameter circles onto baking paper, turn upside down and place on baking trays. Or if you would like to make one large pavlova, trace a 20 cm diameter circle onto a sheet of baking paper. (I like to use a pizza tray instead of a baking tray when making a large pav.)

- Place all of the ingredients in the bowl of a food processor fitted with a whisk attachment and beat on high speed for 20 minutes or until stiff and shiny and tripled in volume. Stop the mixer and scrape down the sides occasionally. Pour the mixture within the circles on the baking paper and smooth the top.

- Bake for 10 minutes on the top oven shelf, then reduce the oven temperature to 100°C and bake for 30 minutes for individual pavlovas or 1 hour for a large pavlova on the bottom shelf. Turn off the oven and leave the pavlovas to completely cool in the oven with the door ajar.

- To make the lemon filling, combine the sugar, cornflour, lemon juice and 1 cup (250 ml) water in a saucepan over medium heat, stirring until the sugar has dissolved and the mixture has thickened. Remove from the heat and quickly stir in the butter and egg yolks. Stir in the dissolved gelatine and allow to cool. Fold in the whipped cream and chill for 30 minutes.

- Spoon the lemon filling onto the pavlovas. Spread the whipped cream over the lemon filling, if desired, and top with your choice of fruit. Chill until serving.

MAKES 6 INDIVIDUAL PAVLOVAS OR SERVES 6 AS A LARGE PAVLOVA

4 eggwhites, at room temperature

1½ cups caster sugar

1 teaspoon cornflour

½ teaspoon vanilla essence

1 teaspoon boiling water

⅓ cup (80 ml) white vinegar

300 ml pouring (thin) cream, whipped, to decorate (optional)

seasonal fruit, to decorate

Lemon filling

¾ cup caster sugar

⅓ cup cornflour

½ cup (125 ml) lemon juice

60 g unsalted butter, diced and softened

3 egg yolks

2 teaspoons powdered gelatine, dissolved in 1 tablespoon boiling water

1 cup lightly whipped cream

Christmas Pudding

It doesn't matter how high the temperature soars on Christmas day, we always have a roast turkey and Mum's mouth-watering pudding. Our family is all from Scottish and English stock – I can't find any Irish in our family tree to add some exotic difference. This Christmas pudding recipe has been handed down from my maternal grandmother. Sadly we don't know where she got it from (maybe her mother?). We do know that she grew up in South London and was a volunteer nurse in Serbia during World War I. She agreed to accompany a friend for a holiday to Australia after the war, and on the journey out, she fell in love with the ship's dashing doctor, who was emigrating from Arbroath, Scotland, on advice from his doctor to live in a warmer climate after being gassed in the war.

The joy of the Christmas pudding has passed through the generations. Granny died in 1986 but she would have loved watching her great-great-grandson appreciating it. When my mother and her sister are together for Christmas and both cook this pudding, their husbands have to be very careful in judging whose is the best – I know the truth. — Jane Jones, Deception Bay, Qld

- Mix the dried fruit, peel, glacé cherries, almonds and brandy in a bowl, cover and leave overnight.

- Cream the butter and sugar in a large bowl until light and fluffy. Add the eggs one at a time, beating well after each addition.

- Add the dried fruit mixture and soaking liquid. Sift in the flour, salt and bicarbonate of soda. Add the breadcrumbs, nutmeg and mixed spice and mix thoroughly.

- Scoop the mixture into a greased 2 litre capacity pudding basin (or two 1 litre capacity ones). Cover with a sheet of greased baking paper and a piece of calico and secure with kitchen string. Steam in a large stockpot for 6 hours – top up the water as necessary. Turn the pudding upside down to drain and leave to completely cool. Store in an airtight container in a cool, dry place (you can make this months before Christmas and it will keep well).

- Steam for 2 hours before serving. Serve with custard or another suitable sauce.

SERVES 8–10

250 g raisins

250 g currants

250 g sultanas

60 g chopped candied peel

60 g glacé cherries

60 g chopped almonds

3 tablespoons brandy or rum

250 g unsalted butter, softened

250 g soft brown sugar

5 eggs, at room temperature

125 g plain flour

pinch of table salt

¼ teaspoon bicarbonate of soda

125 g fresh breadcrumbs

¼ teaspoon ground nutmeg

¼ teaspoon mixed spice

custard or your favourite sauce, to serve

Mum's Rice Pudding

This has to be the cheapest, easiest and most comforting dessert ever created. My mum grew up with it, and my brother and I still request she makes it for us every time we go home. There's a story in our family that one of my great aunts made it for my great uncle to welcome him home back from the war, unfortunately he'd had enough rice in the Changi prisoner of war camp to last him a lifetime and it wasn't well received. But the family recipe is still loved to this day. Opinions are divided on whether you avoid the skin that forms on the top as completely inedible (me) or the best part of the pudding (my brother). You can also add rhubarb, cream, cinnamon, or just about anything that takes your fancy. — Leila McKinnon

- Preheat the oven to 140°C and grease six 150 ml capacity ramekins or a 1 litre capacity baking dish with the butter.

- Divide the rice, sugar and milk evenly among the ramekins and give each a little stir. If making one large pudding, add the rice, sugar and milk to the baking dish and stir to combine.

- Cover with foil and bake for 40 minutes for individual ramekins or 2 hours for a large pudding. Give it a stir halfway through the cooking time. Remove the foil for the last 10 minutes of cooking if you like a browned top.

- Serve with stewed or poached fruit.

MAKES 6

20 g unsalted butter

2½ tablespoons white rice

1 tablespoon white or soft brown sugar, or to taste

1 litre milk

stewed or poached fruit, to serve

Tiramisu

This recipe was given to me by my Italian auntie when I was living in Italy. She 'borrowed' the recipe from a Roman cafe that was well known in our area for their amazing desserts, particularly their delicious tiramisu. I'm not exactly sure how she managed to extract their secret formula. I like to think she won them over with the story of her only niece (me) leaving the country forever and going to live on the other side of the world (Australia) and wanting to give me something sweet to remember my good times in Italy. Every time I make it, I think of my auntie and our time together in Italy enjoying fine food.

Anyone who has ever tasted this tiramisu has loved it – even those who do not normally like coffee are converted. It is simple to make, absolutely delicious, and so creamy, you can feel it going straight for your hips! — Karen Fellus, Maroubra, NSW

- Brush the base of a large glass bowl (at least 2 litre capacity) or a 20 x 20 cm dish around 5 cm deep with some of the coffee, then dust with cocoa. Set aside.

- Combine the remaining coffee with the liqueur in a shallow dish.

- Beat the egg yolks and sugar in a large bowl until light and fluffy, then fold in the mascarpone.

- Beat the eggwhites until stiff peaks form, then gently fold into the mascarpone mixture.

- Dip the biscuits one by one in the coffee mixture, ensuring each is well soaked, and arrange a single layer in the prepared bowl. Dust with cocoa, then add a layer of the mascarpone mixture and dust with cocoa again. Repeat layering the biscuits, dusting with cocoa and layering the mascarpone mixture, until they are all used up, making sure you finish with the mascarpone mixture covered with a generous dusting of cocoa.

- Refrigerate for at least 4 hours or overnight before serving.

SERVES 8–12

8 espresso coffees
sifted bitter cocoa powder
  (I use Van Houten), for dusting
coffee liqueur or Baileys (optional)
4 eggs, separated
⅓ cup caster sugar
500 g good-quality mascarpone
500 g packet savoiardi biscuits

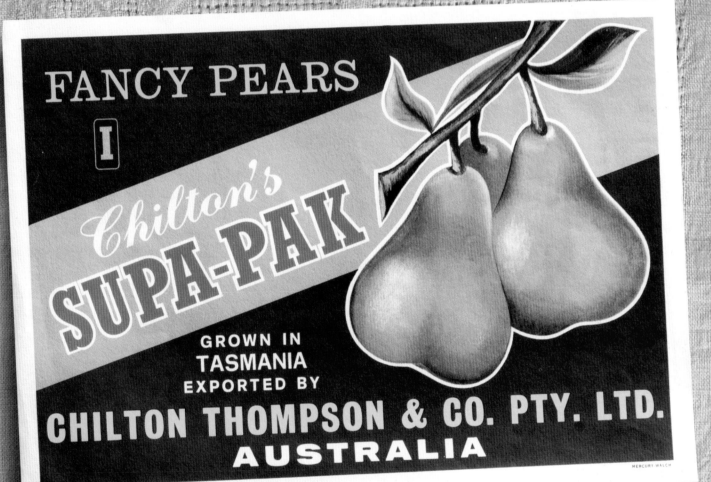

Lemon Cheesecake

I make this cheesecake all the time for my family. It's so easy to put together and doesn't require any specialist baking equipment. Make sure you use good-quality lemons and don't skimp on the juice – nothing's more important than the citrus tang that offsets all the cheesy goodness. — Jen Tickle, Castlemaine, Vic.

- Place the crushed biscuits, ground ginger and melted butter in a bowl and mix well. Press the mixture into the base and up the sides of a greased 20 cm springform cake tin. Refrigerate until firm.

- Beat the cream cheese and cream together until completely smooth. Gradually beat in the condensed milk, then enough lemon juice, 1 teaspoon at a time, to reach a thick consistency.

- Pour the cream cheese mixture into the biscuit shell and refrigerate for at least 24 hours before serving.

- Top with whipped cream and fresh fruit to serve.

SERVES 8

250 g plain sweet biscuits, finely crushed

½ teaspoon ground ginger

125 g unsalted butter, melted and slightly cooled

250 g cream cheese, softened

⅓ cup pouring (single) cream

400 g sweetened condensed milk

3 tablespoons lemon juice

whipped cream and fresh fruit of your choice, to decorate

Green Pudding

It was a winter's night in Melbourne in 1975 and my sister Jane was bringing her first boyfriend, Trevor, home for dinner. There was much excitement in an all-sister household – males were rare beings (just the dog – oh, and Dad) – and as Jane is the eldest, it was the first time a real live 'boyfriend' had dined with us. Being a rather annoying youngest sister, I was fixated on Trevor and didn't hide my scrutiny. But then something else got my attention … I tasted the most fantastic dessert ever. Mum thinks she got the recipe from the *Age* newspaper, my middle sister Liz suggested it might have been on the back of a cornflakes packet, but who cares – it was gorgeous! I've been obsessed with this dessert for the past 37 years and insist on having it every year for my birthday, as does Liz. Jane now makes it for her family too – it's a hit with her grandson – but it just doesn't taste the same as when Mum makes it. There is something about the zingy lime cream combined with the crunchy chocolate that is irresistible. (It didn't work out with Trevor, though; Jane went on to marry Steve, and he loves green pudding too.) — Cate Paterson, Bondi, NSW

- Melt the butter and golden syrup in a frying pan over low heat and stir to combine.

- Place the cornflakes and melted chocolate in a large bowl, add the butter mixture and gently combine. Gently press into the base of 8 small glasses or a 20 cm pie dish. Leave to set.

- Meanwhile, make the filling. Dissolve the jelly crystals in the boiling water in a large heatproof bowl. Set aside to cool. Whisk the evaporated milk until thick and frothy, then combine with the cooled jelly.

- Pour the filling into the glasses or pie shell and refrigerate for about 3 hours or until the filling is set.

- To serve, decorate with whipped cream, edible flowers and lime zest if desired.

SERVES 8

20 g unsalted butter
2 tablespoons golden syrup
125 g cornflakes
90 g dark chocolate, melted
whipped cream, edible flowers and lime zest, to decorate (optional)

Filling
85 g packet lime jelly crystals
210 ml boiling water
220 ml evaporated milk, chilled

Lemon Delicious

My mum used to make this every Sunday when her mum, Gran, would visit. This pudding reminds me of winter in Wagga Wagga, in New South Wales, and happy afternoons spent with them and my sister. — Maria Naidoo, Fairfield, Victoria

- Preheat the oven to 180°C and grease a 2 litre capacity baking dish.

- Combine the flour, sugar and lemon zest in a large bowl.

- Add the lemon juice, melted butter and egg yolks and beat until thoroughly mixed. Gradually stir in the milk.

- Beat the eggwhites until stiff peaks form, then gently fold into the flour mixture.

- Pour into the prepared dish, place in a roasting tray and fill with cold water until it reaches halfway up the sides of the dish.

- Bake for 40 minutes or until golden brown

- Serve immediately with ice-cream or cream.

SERVES 6

½ cup self-raising flour, sifted

1 cup caster sugar

finely grated zest of 1 large lemon

⅓ cup (80 ml) lemon juice

80 g unsalted butter, melted and slightly cooled

3 eggs, at room temperature, separated

1½ (375 ml) cups milk

ice-cream or cream, to serve

Margaret's Berry Meringue Cake

This delicious dessert is a cross between two much-loved desserts – the iconic pavlova and the vacherin. It is simply luscious. – Margaret Fulton, Balmain, NSW

- Preheat the oven to 200–210°C. Trace a 22 cm diameter circle onto each of two sheets of baking paper, turn upside down and place on 2 baking trays.

- Place the eggwhites and salt in the bowl of a food processor fitted with a whisk attachment and whisk until stiff peaks form. Gradually sprinkle in the sugar, 1 tablespoon at a time, whisking on high speed until all the sugar has been added and the mixture is stiff and shiny.

- Gently fold in the vinegar and vanilla extract. Spoon large dollops inside the circles on the baking paper and lightly smooth over the tops.

- Place in the oven, immediately reduce the temperature to 150°C and bake for 1 hour. Turn off the oven and leave the meringues to completely cool in the oven. (If using a gas oven, bake at 150°C for 1 hour, then reduce the oven temperature to 120°C and bake for another 30 minutes before turning off the oven and leaving to cool in the oven.)

- Remove the meringues from the oven and remove the baking paper. Don't worry if the meringues collapse slightly or if there are cracks on the surface. Slide one meringue onto a cake stand or serving platter. Spread half of the whipped cream over the meringue, top with half of the berries, then top with the other meringue and remaining cream and berries. Dust with icing sugar to serve.

SERVES 8–10

4 eggwhites

pinch of table salt

1½ cups caster sugar, sifted

1½ teaspoons white vinegar

1 teaspoon vanilla extract

300 ml pouring (thin) cream, whipped

mixed fresh berries (strawberries hulled and halved), to decorate

sifted icing sugar, for dusting

Ash's Chocolate Mousse

I have a beautiful wife and three wonderful kids: Chloe, seven years old; Laura, two years old; and Adam, eighteen months old. In my spare time I love to cook and my favourite thing to make is my choc mousse. The kids love to help me make it and lick the bowl and spoon.
— Ashley Pagotto, South Lismore, NSW

- Beat the cream cheese, sugar and egg together in a large bowl until combined and smooth.

- Melt the chopped chocolate in a heatproof bowl placed over a saucepan of barely simmering water. Stir occasionally until melted and smooth.

- Add to the cream cheese mixture and beat until well combined.

- Gently fold in the whipped cream until combined.

- Spoon into small glasses or bowls and refrigerate until chilled and set.

- Garnish with the grated chocolate to serve.

SERVES 6–8

125 g cream cheese, softened

½ cup white sugar

1 egg, at room temperature

250 g milk cooking chocolate, roughly chopped, plus extra grated, to garnish

600 ml thickened (whipping) cream, lightly whipped

Pears with Port

Usually I serve much less sophisticated desserts, such as Eton mess or banana split, but these pears with port are just a little more grand for when entertaining. They look beautiful served in a gorgeous glass, such as a brandy balloon, and the orange and cinnamon flavours are especially appropriate in winter or during the festive season. — Annette Pedersen, Radcliffe, Qld

- Dry the pear quarters well. Melt the butter in a large frying pan over low heat, add the pear quarters, coat in the butter and cook for 4–5 minutes or until coloured and beginning to soften. Avoid handling the pears too much.

- Add the sugar and cook until it begins to bubble and caramelise, then remove from the heat and add the cinnamon, orange zest, port and orange juice. Return to the heat, bring to the boil and cook for 5 minutes or until the sauce has slightly thickened.

- Divide the pear quarters among bowls, spoon over some of the sauce and serve with whipped cream.

SERVES 6

6 small ripe but firm pears, peeled, cored and quartered

60 g unsalted butter

½ cup firmly packed soft brown sugar

1 teaspoon ground cinnamon

2 teaspoons grated orange zest

½ cup (125 ml) port

½ cup (125 ml) orange juice

whipped cream, to serve

Pat's Trifle

This was originally my mother's recipe – I have altered it a little over the years. Now I am a great-grandmother and it is my job to make the trifle for the Christmas table. I love how the slices of Swiss roll make a beautiful pattern around the edge of the bowl. It's the perfect festive treat! — Pat Tompkins, Cherrybrook, NSW

- Make the jelly according to the packet directions and refrigerate until set.

- Slice the sponge roll into 12–14 slices and use to line the base and sides of a 1.5 litre capacity glass bowl.

- Drizzle over the sherry, scatter over the coconut and arrange the fruit salad and strawberries over the top.

- Cut the jelly into small pieces (I like to use a fork to break up it into chunks). Spread the jelly over the fruit.

- Cover the jelly with the custard, agitate slightly so the custard fills the gaps and smooth over the top.

- Sprinkle with a little nutmeg and refrigerate for at least 1 hour to set.

- Top with the whipped cream and almonds to serve.

SERVES 8

85 g packet port wine jelly crystals

1 store-bought jam sponge roll

3 tablespoons sweet sherry
  or brandy, or to taste

1 tablespoon desiccated coconut

400 g can fruit salad, drained

125 g strawberries, hulled
  and halved (optional)

600 g custard

pinch of ground nutmeg

1½ cups thickened (whipping)
  cream, whipped

slivered almonds, toasted,
  to garnish

Lemon Sorbet

I've toyed with every flavour of sorbet from apple to white nectarine, but I don't think I'm alone in always returning to lemon. It's the perfect dessert for a sizzling Australian summer: icy cold, sweet, tangy and not too filling. It's also a great dish that can be made the day before a dinner or an occasion. — Reuben Quinn, East St Kilda, Victoria

- Place the sugar and 2 cups (500 ml) water in a small saucepan over low heat and stir constantly until the sugar has dissolved. Bring to the boil and cook for 5 minutes. Remove from the heat and add the lemon juice and zest. Set aside to cool.

- Strain the mixture into a rectangular metal tin and freeze until set.

- Beat the eggwhite until soft peaks form, then gradually beat in the extra sugar until it has dissolved.

- Break the frozen mixture into chunks in a large bowl and beat with hand-held electric beaters until smooth. Fold in the beaten eggwhite, then return to the metal tin and freeze until set.

- To serve, scoop the sorbet into chilled glasses. Store in the freezer, covered, for up to 2 days.

MAKES ABOUT 1 LITRE

1 cup caster sugar, plus
　1 tablespoon extra

½ cup (125 ml) lemon juice

1 teaspoon finely grated
　lemon zest

1 eggwhite

1 tablespoon caster sugar

CAKES

Lamingtons

To me treats don't get any better or any more Australian than a lamington and a cuppa. There's a reason we've based more than a hundred years of community fundraising around this chocolate–coconut treat – they're just too good. Although they are perfect on their own, I serve mine with a blob of jam and a few spoonfuls of cream. — Sinia Deakin, Miami, Qld

- Preheat the oven to 180°C and grease a 28 cm x 18 cm lamington tin.

- Cream the butter and sugar until light and fluffy. Beat in the eggs one at a time, beating well after each addition.

- Fold in the flour alternately with the combined milk and vanilla essence. Pour the mixture into the prepared tin.

- Bake for 30–40 minutes or until golden and a skewer inserted into the centre comes out clean.

- Remove from the oven, cool in the tin for 5 minutes, then turn out onto a wire rack and leave to completely cool. Ideally, store the cake in an airtight container for 1–2 days before cutting and icing, as the day-old cake will be less crumbly.

- To make the icing, place the butter in a large heatproof bowl, pour over the boiling water, add the cocoa and mix well. Beat in the icing sugar until the mixture is smooth.

- Cut the cake into 5.5 cm squares.

- Place the coconut on a plate. Using a long-pronged fork, dip the cake squares into the icing, then roll in the coconut and place on a wire rack for the icing to set.

MAKES 15

125 g unsalted butter, softened
¾ cup caster sugar
2 eggs, at room temperature
2 cups self-raising flour, sifted
½ cup (125 ml) milk
½ teaspoon vanilla essence

Icing
30 g unsalted butter, softened
3–4 tablespoons boiling water
2 tablespoons cocoa powder
2 cups icing sugar, sifted
2 cups shredded coconut

Persian Love Cake

I love this cake not only for its name, but it also has the most complex flavours of any cake I've tasted. Exotic and sophisticated, this is the cake for lovers. In fact I'm told the baker should think about love when rubbing the mixture together. I like to warm it slightly before serving with super-rich cream – don't be afraid to indulge. — Jayneeta Govender, Narre Warren, Victoria

- Preheat the oven to 180°C and grease a 26 cm cake tin.

- Combine the almond meal, sugars, butter and salt in a large bowl and, using your fingertips, rub until a breadcrumb texture forms. Spoon half of the mixture into the prepared tin, gently pressing to evenly cover the base. Set aside.

- Add the eggs, yoghurt and nutmeg to the remaining almond meal mixture and beat with a wooden spoon until smooth and creamy. Pour over the prepared base, smooth the top and scatter the pistachios around the edge.

- Bake for 30–35 minutes or until golden and set.

- Remove from the oven and cool in the tin. Decorate with rose petals and serve with yoghurt on the side.

SERVES 8

3 cups almond meal

1 cup raw sugar

1 cup firmly packed soft brown sugar

120 g unsalted butter, softened

1 teaspoon table salt

2 eggs, lightly beaten

1 cup plain yoghurt, plus extra, to serve

1 teaspoon freshly ground nutmeg

3 tablespoons pistachios, finely chopped

unsprayed rose petals, to decorate

Rosie's Banana Cake

Twenty years ago my mum was searching for the perfect cake recipe for her three kids who weren't big on sweets. We loved our fruit, though, bananas in particular, and so began our family's love affair with this banana cake. Even today whenever we have a family get-together and Mum asks what kind of cake she should make, the answer is always banana cake. It's just that good. And there are never leftovers. The beauty of this recipe is in its simplicity – it's honest, easy home cooking at its very best. It's the kind of food that makes me think of family and being together. — Bec Donnelly, Fortitude Valley, Qld

- Preheat the oven to 150°C. Grease a 23 cm square cake tin and a 23 cm x 13 cm loaf tin and line both with baking paper.

- Sift the flour and bicarbonate of soda into a large bowl and make a well in the centre.

- Stir in the sugar, eggs, banana and oil and mix until smooth. Pour the mixture into the prepared tins.

- Bake for about 45 minutes for the loaf and 1½ hours for the cake or until a skewer inserted into the centre comes out clean.

- Remove from the oven and leave to cool in the tins for 10 minutes, then turn out onto wire racks to completely cool.

- To make the icing, beat the icing sugar, butter, cream cheese, apricot jam and vanilla essence in a large bowl until light and fluffy. Set aside at room temperature until needed.

- Spread the icing over the cooled cakes.

- Store leftovers in an airtight container in the fridge but bring to room temperature before serving.

MAKES 1 SQUARE CAKE AND 1 LOAF / SERVES ABOUT 30

2½ cups self-raising flour

1 teaspoon bicarbonate of soda

1 cup caster sugar

4 eggs, lightly beaten

2½ cups mashed ripe banana (about 5 large)

1 cup (250 ml) vegetable oil

Icing

2 cups icing sugar, sifted

60 g unsalted butter, softened

100 g cream cheese, softened

1 tablespoon apricot jam

1 teaspoon vanilla essence

Lemon Yoghurt Cake

This is one of the quickest, most fuss-free cake recipes around. I love the springy lightness of its texture and the sweet tanginess of the flavour. And because it uses yoghurt I like to think of it as almost healthy. Even my dad, who thinks spices and yoghurt have no business anywhere near a cake, loves this recipe. It tastes superb served with yoghurt, too. — Leila McKinnon

- Preheat the oven to 190°C. Grease a 23 cm round cake tin and line with baking paper.

- Cream the butter, caster sugar and lemon zest in a large bowl until light and fluffy. Beat in the brown sugar and lemon essence. Beat in the eggs one at a time, beating well after each addition, and continue to beat for 3–4 minutes.

- Sift the flour, salt and spice together into a bowl.

- Fold the flour mixture and yoghurt alternately into the butter mixture. Pour into the prepared tin.

- Bake for 45 minutes or until a skewer inserted into the centre comes out clean.

- Remove from the oven and leave to cool in the tin for 3 minutes, then turn out onto a wire rack to cool completely.

- Decorate with lemon slices if desired.

SERVES 8

185 g unsalted butter, softened

1 cup caster sugar

1 tablespoon finely grated lemon zest

¾ cup firmly packed soft brown sugar

1 teaspoon lemon essence

3 eggs, at room temperature

2¼ cups self-raising flour

¼ teaspoon table salt

1 teaspoon mixed spice

1 cup plain yoghurt

lemon slices cooked in sugar syrup, to decorate (optional)

Victoria Sponge Sandwich

I like to put on a pinny, channel my grandma and whip up this old-fashioned favourite for a dose of sweet nostalgia. It looks much more difficult than it is. Whatever you do, do not destroy that illusion! Which jam you use is up to you, but I prefer to use one that's not too sweet – a slightly tart fruit offsets the sugary cake and rich cream perfectly. — Maria Wassef, Panania, NSW

- Preheat the oven to 180°C. Grease two 20 cm round sandwich cake tins and line with baking paper.

- Cream the butter and sugar until light and fluffy. Beat in the eggs one at a time, beating well after each addition. Mix in the vanilla essence.

- Sift in the flour and gently fold in. Divide the mixture equally between the prepared tins.

- Bake for 20–25 minutes or until well risen and golden and the centre springs back when touched.

- Remove from the oven and cool in the tins for 5 minutes, then turn out onto a wire rack, remove the baking paper and leave to cool completely.

- Place one cake on a serving platter, spread with jam, then cream and sandwich together with the other cake. Dust with icing sugar.

SERVES 8

125 g unsalted butter, softened
½ cup caster sugar
2 eggs, at room temperature
few drops vanilla essence
1 cup self-raising flour
strawberry jam, to fill
whipped cream, to fill
sifted icing sugar, for dusting

Fruit Cake No.1

This recipe is handed down from my nan, Eileen Mary Best, my mother's mother, a typist for the American Army based in Sydney during World War II who married a soldier. We don't know where Nan found this recipe, but it is written in her recipe book as Fruit Cake No.#1. Nan used to make about ten of these at Christmas to give as gifts to each of the children's teachers, to the neighbours, and one for the family too.

I remember making Nan's fruit cake on school Christmas holidays with her watchful eye on me at all times making sure that I was doing it right – lining the baking tin with baking paper and creaming the butter and sugar were very important steps. Nan has since passed away but when we cook her fruit cake, our family has wonderful memories of what it represents. It's the cake of joy and love. — Michelle Thrift, Balaclava, Victoria

- Preheat the oven to 125°C. Grease a 20 cm square or round cake tin and double-line the base and sides with brown paper (or foil butter wrappers).

- Cream the butter, sugar, spices and coffee essence together until light and fluffy. Add the beaten egg one-fifth at a time, beating well after each addition.

- Add ½ cup of the plain flour and mix through. Add the remaining plain flour, then the self-raising flour, mixing after each addition. Fold through the dried fruit and almonds. Pour into the prepared tin.

- Bake for 3 hours. If the cake looks like it is getting too coloured in the last 30 minutes of baking, reduce the oven temperature to 100°C.

- Remove from the oven and pour over the wine. Turn the oven off, return the cake to the oven and leave to completely cool.

SERVES 16

250 g unsalted butter, softened

1 cup caster sugar

1 teaspoon mixed spice

1 teaspoon ground cinnamon

1 teaspoon ground nutmeg

1 tablespoon coffee essence

5 eggs (60 g each), at room temperature, lightly beaten

1½ cups plain flour, sifted

1 heaped cup self-raising flour, sifted

750 g mixed dried fruit

60 g blanched almonds

½ cup (125 ml) wine, sweet sherry or brandy

Chocolate Cake

This is just a simple chocolate cake that my family has made for years, but chocolate doesn't need any help – it's just fine on its own. This recipe isn't much more complicated than using a packet cake mix, but it is incredibly moist and the vanilla essence makes a big difference to the flavour. — Paul Adshead, West Brunswick, Vic.

- Preheat the oven to 180°C. Grease a 20 cm ring cake tin (7 cm depth) and line with baking paper.

- Cream the butter and sugar until light and fluffy. Mix in the vanilla essence. Beat the eggs in one at a time, beating well after each addition.

- Sift the flour, bicarbonate of soda and cocoa together into a bowl.

- Fold the flour mixture and milk alternately into the butter mixture. Pour into the prepared tin.

- Bake for 45 minutes or until a skewer inserted into the centre comes out clean.

- Remove from the oven and cool in the tin for 15 minutes, then turn out onto a wire rack and leave to cool completely.

- Ice the sides and top of the cake and decorate with strawberries.

SERVES 8

125 g unsalted butter, softened

½ cup caster sugar

1 teaspoon vanilla essence

2 eggs, at room temperature

2 cups self-raising flour

½ teaspoon bicarbonate of soda

⅓ cup cocoa powder

150 ml milk

store-bought chocolate frosting, to ice

strawberries (halved if large), to decorate

Gingerbread

You can buy all the gingerbread you like but none will taste better than this amazing recipe I have been making since I was little, especially fresh from the oven. The ground ginger, mixed spices and golden syrup make this version sing and fill my house with the most intoxicating aromas. — Louise Macri, Crows Nest, NSW

- Preheat the oven to 190°C. Grease a 25 cm x 13 cm x 8 cm loaf tin and line with baking paper.

- Sift the flour, salt and bicarbonate of soda into a large bowl and add the ginger and mixed spice.

- Rub the butter into the flour with your fingertips. Mix in the sugar.

- Lightly beat the egg and combine with the golden syrup and milk. Pour into the flour mixture and mix quickly and lightly into a soft batter until just combined. Pour into the prepared tin.

- Bake for 30–40 minutes or until a skewer inserted into the centre comes out clean.

- Remove from the oven and turn out onto a wire rack to cool.

- Enjoy spread with butter.

SERVES 6

2 ½ cups plain flour

pinch of table salt

1 teaspoon bicarbonate of soda

1 tablespoon ground ginger

½ teaspoon mixed spice

125 g unsalted butter, diced

¾ cup firmly packed soft brown sugar

1 egg, at room temperature

⅓ cup golden syrup or treacle

1 cup (250 ml) milk

butter, to serve

Nonna's Pound Cake

This recipe came out from Italy with my grandmother and has since been made by three generations. The recipe is simple to remember and it is the cake I always turn to when I don't have access to a cookbook. You can also make muffins or a loaf or add dried fruit to it.
— Loretta Fincato, East Hills, NSW

- Preheat the oven to 180°C. Grease a 22 cm round cake tin and line with baking paper.

- Sift the flour and salt into a large bowl, mix in the sugar and make a well in the centre.

- Add the oil, milk, eggs, vanilla extract and lemon juice to the well in the flour mixture and beat with hand-held electric beaters until smooth and combined.

- Fold in the sultanas and pour into the prepared tin.

- Bake for 40 minutes or until a skewer inserted into the centre comes out clean.

- Remove from the oven and cool in the tin for 10 minutes, then turn out and cool on a wire rack.

SERVES 8–10

2 cups self-raising flour
small pinch of table salt
¾ cup caster sugar
½ cup (125 ml) vegetable oil
½ cup (125 ml) milk
2 eggs, at room temperature
1 teaspoon vanilla extract
juice of 1 lemon
1 cup sultanas (see Note)

Note

You can replace the sultanas with ½ cup walnuts and ½ cup grated carrot.

Muriel's Fruit Loaf

Muriel McCabe is an amazing lady. She's dedicated much of her time over the past 30 years to Legacy, as one of their tireless volunteers who provide support to Australian Defence Force families needing support. I think what makes Muriel's Fruit Loaf so special is the cup of coconut, it's this easy sprinkling of exotica that transforms an ordinary Aussie snack into one that wakes up the palate and has you wondering if it's impolite to ask for the recipe. Don't stint on the butter when serving. — Leila McKinnon

- Preheat the oven to 180°C. Grease a 25 cm x 13 cm x 6 cm loaf tin and line with baking paper.

- Combine the flour and sugar in a large bowl. Stir in the milk, then fold in the dried fruit and coconut. Pour into the prepared tin.

- Bake for 45 minutes or until a skewer inserted into the centre comes out clean.

- Remove from the oven and cool in the tin for 10 minutes, then turn out onto a wire rack and leave to cool.

- Slice and enjoy spread with butter. This is best eaten on the day of making.

SERVES 6

1 cup self-raising flour, sifted
1 cup white sugar
¾ cup (180 ml) milk
250 g packet mixed dried fruit
1 cup desiccated coconut
butter, to serve

Biscuits
Slices & Treats

Sandy's Rocky Road

I've been making this recipe for the past 20 years. It is a favourite of my teenagers, son Mitchael and daughter Jordan. Jordan has recently begun making it for her friends, and I'm certain the recipe will be passed along for more generations to come. — Sandy Kiely, North Curl Curl, NSW

- Line a large baking tray with baking paper.

- Melt the chocolate in a heatproof bowl over a saucepan of barely simmering water, stirring occasionally, until smooth.

- Combine the marshmallows, raspberries, almonds and coconut (if using) in a large bowl and stir to distribute evenly.

- Add the chocolate to the marshmallow mixture and stir to coat everything well in the chocolate. While still warm, spread onto the prepared tray to about the thickness of a marshmallow. Refrigerate until set.

- Cut into pieces to serve.

MAKES ENOUGH FOR 2 CHOCOHOLICS OR 8 NON-CHOCOHOLICS

500 g plain milk chocolate, broken into pieces

250 g pink and white marshmallows, halved

90 g raspberry jelly lollies, halved

100 g slivered almonds, toasted

½ cup desiccated coconut (optional)

Kanafeh (Sweet Buttery Ricotta Slice)

I love this dessert. It's best eaten still warm from the oven. The combination of sweet floral syrup, crunchy pastry and creamy ricotta is irresistible and you'll find it's perfect when you want something sweet but not too heavy. My aunty made it for me for the first time more than 25 years ago and whenever I eat it, it always reminds me of her. — Maria Karotos, Keilor East, Victoria

- Preheat the oven to 180°C.

- Crumble the kataifi with your fingers into a large bowl, making sure there are no clumps. Add the melted butter and mix well so that the butter coats all of the kataifi. Place half of the mixture in a 25 cm square cake tin (or a 30 cm x 20 cm rectangular one) and evenly spread to line the base. Press down gently with your hands.

- Combine the ricotta and mozzarella in a large bowl and set aside.

- Heat the milk in a small saucepan over medium heat for 1 minute, then add the semolina and cook for 30 seconds, whisking to form a paste. Add to the cheese mixture and combine well. Pour the mixture on top of the kataifi in the tin and evenly spread. Cover with the remaining kataifi mixture.

- Bake for 45 minutes or until golden.

- Meanwhile, make the syrup. Combine the sugar with 1 cup (250 ml) water in a small saucepan over medium–high heat and bring to the boil, stirring to dissolve the sugar. Cook for 5 minutes, stir in the lemon juice, rosewater and orange blossom water, then remove from the heat and set aside to cool to room temperature.

- Remove the slice from the oven, drizzle over the syrup and set aside for 30 minutes to absorb. Serve warm, garnished with the pistachios.

Note

- Kataifi pastry is available from Middle Eastern grocery stores and Greek bakeries.

SERVES 12

375 g kataifi pastry (shredded filo dough) (see Note)

150 g unsalted butter, melted and slightly cooled

500 g ricotta

250 g shredded mozzarella

1 cup (250 ml) milk

½ cup semolina

finely chopped pistachios or walnuts, to garnish

Syrup

1 cup white sugar

1 tablespoon lemon juice

½ tablespoon rosewater

½ tablespoon orange blossom water

Stef's Chocolate Kisses

This is my aunt's old family recipe that I've adapted and made my own. These go wonderfully with a cup of tea or coffee, and make a great little gift to bring to someone's house for dessert. You can try using different nuts too. I sometimes like to use hazelnuts (with their skins rubbed off) or pistachios. — Stefanie Sgroi, Russell Lea, NSW

- Combine the hazelnut–chocolate spread and almonds in a bowl and mix well. Using damp hands, roll the mixture into walnut-sized balls and place on a tray lined with baking paper. Refrigerate (do not freeze) for about 30 minutes for the balls to firm up.

- Melt the chocolate in a heatproof bowl over a saucepan of barely simmering water, stirring occasionally, until smooth. Once melted, remove from the heat.

- Using a fork, dip the balls into the melted chocolate and place back on the tray.

- Refrigerate for about 2 hours for the chocolate to set. Store in an airtight container in the refrigerator but bring to room temperature before eating.

MAKES ABOUT 50

375 g hazelnut–chocolate spread

500 g roasted unsalted almonds, finely chopped

300 g dark cooking chocolate, broken into pieces

Banana Choc Chip Mini Muffins

I have always liked to cook and bake since I was young, especially when I was a teenager and my mum would allow me the run of the kitchen. She is a great cook, especially with her European background, and was always giving me great cooking tips. These mini muffins are always a hit among the kids – and adults – at my mothers' group meetings. Their size makes them great for children and they can be easily tucked into lunchboxes. — Susan Shanta, Seaford, Victoria

- Preheat the oven to 180°C and line mini-muffin tins with cupcake papers.

- Sift the flour, baking powder and bicarbonate of soda into a large bowl, add the sugar and cinnamon and stir to distribute evenly. Make a well in the centre.

- Add the melted butter, egg and milk to the well in the flour mixture and gently mix until just combined.

- Gently fold in the mashed banana and chocolate chips and mix through.

- Spoon into the muffin tins, making sure to fill the cupcake papers only two-thirds full.

- Bake for 10 minutes or until golden.

- Remove from the oven and cool in the tins for 10 minutes, then turn out onto wire racks to cool.

- Dust with icing sugar to serve.

MAKES ABOUT 35

2 cups self-raising flour

2½ teaspoons baking powder

¼ teaspoon bicarbonate of soda

¾ cup caster sugar

½ teaspoon ground cinnamon

2 tablespoons unsalted butter, melted and slightly cooled

1 egg, at room temperature

3 tablespoons milk

½ cup mashed banana

½ cup milk chocolate chips

sifted icing sugar, for dusting

Chocolate Weet-Bix Slice

This is a great slice to have on hand when unexpected guests with kids drop by. It keeps well in an airtight container in the cupboard. I used to pack it in my children's luggage when they started term at boarding school and hope that it reminded them of home. It's always the first thing they asked me to make when they came back home. — Margaret Hendriks, Mollymook, NSW

- Preheat the oven to 180°C. Grease an 18 cm square cake tin and line with baking paper.

- Sift the flour and cocoa powder into a large bowl. Add the Weet-Bix, coconut and sugar and stir to distribute evenly.

- Add the butter and vanilla essence and mix well. Press into the prepared tin.

- Bake for 10–12 minutes. Remove from the oven and cool in the tin for 10 minutes, then turn out onto a wire rack.

- To make the icing, sift the icing sugar and cocoa powder into a bowl. Add the butter and enough boiling water, a tablespoon at a time, to make a thick icing consistency.

- Ice the slice while still warm. Leave to cool to room temperature for the icing to set.

SERVES 6–8

1 cup self-raising flour

1 tablespoon cocoa powder

4 Weet-Bix, finely crushed

½ cup desiccated coconut

½ cup loosely packed soft brown sugar

140 g unsalted butter, melted and slightly cooled

1 teaspoon vanilla essence

Icing

1 cup icing sugar

1 tablespoon cocoa powder

20 g unsalted butter, melted and slightly cooled

boiling water

Anzac Biscuits

When we were growing up Dad worked several jobs and restored cars for sale during his time off, so it was pretty rare and very exciting to spend time with him in the kitchen. When he did get time, he took it very seriously and made these biscuits. He favoured a very chewy kind of Anzac. The biscuits will be affected by different brands of oats and syrup, so experiment with them until you get the right amount of chew. — Leila McKinnon

- Preheat the oven to 180°C and grease two large baking trays.

- Combine the oats, coconut, flour and sugar in a large bowl and stir to distribute evenly.

- Melt the butter and golden syrup together in a small saucepan over low heat. Remove from the heat.

- Dissolve the bicarbonate of soda in the boiling water and add to the butter mixture. Add to the dry ingredients and combine well.

- Place 1 tablespoon amounts of the mixture onto the prepared trays, allowing room to spread between each.

- Bake for 15 minutes or until golden.

- Remove from the oven and cool for 5 minutes on the trays, then move to wire racks to cool completely.

MAKES ABOUT 30

¾ cup rolled oats

⅔ cup desiccated coconut

½ cup plain flour, sifted

⅓ cup caster sugar

50 g unsalted butter

1 tablespoon golden syrup

½ teaspoon bicarbonate of soda

2 tablespoons boiling water

Scotch Shortbread

My grandmother was a pastrycook in Scotland. She came to Australia, married a Tasmanian, lived in Sydney, and this was her favourite recipe. It's so easy and has been passed down through our family. It's a must when there is a family gathering. — Madeline Meyn, Tumbi Umbi, NSW

- Preheat the oven to 150–160°C and grease a 25 cm pie dish.

- Cream the butter and sugar in a large bowl until light and fluffy.

- Sift in the flour and gently fold in.

- Gently press the mixture into the prepared tray, making sure the top is even. Press the edges with your thumb to decorate and prick all over with a fork.

- Bake for about 30 minutes or until lightly golden.

- Remove from the oven and while still warm cut into about 12 wedges. Sprinkle the top with sugar. Leave to cool in the tin.

MAKES ABOUT 12

170 g unsalted butter, softened

90 g caster sugar, plus extra, for sprinkling

250 g plain flour

Pastatelle (Southern Italian Pastries)

I'm a children's cookbook author and I credit my love of food to my nonna and mum, both of whom taught me how to cook as a child. My Nonna Carmela taught Mum to make pastatelle when she was younger. Mum then passed the recipe onto me. Our family has been making these for more than 50 years, always on Christmas Eve. The mere thought of them instantly transports me back to my childhood. They're usually served as large pastatelle; however, I've modernised the recipe and turned them into little petits fours. They can be served any time of the year alongside a coffee at the end of a meal. — Sabrina Parrini, Romsey, Victoria

- To make the filling, cook the chestnuts in a large saucepan of boiling water for 4 hours or until soft to the bite, topping up the water if necessary. Drain and process, in batches, in a food processor until a very smooth paste. If it tastes grainy, you may need to pass it through a mouli. Combine with the remaining ingredients in a large bowl and mix well. Set aside.

- Combine the strong flour, eggs, wine and oil in a large bowl and mix to form a dough. Turn out onto a lightly floured work surface and knead for 10 minutes or until smooth and elastic. Divide into 9 pieces.

- Lightly flour a pasta machine and work surface. Working with one piece of dough at a time and lightly flouring as you go, feed each piece through the pasta machine, beginning on setting 1 and working through to setting 5 until the dough sheet is about 3 mm thick.

- Place the dough sheet on the floured surface. Place 1 teaspoon amounts of filling along the centre line of the sheet, about 1 cm apart. Gently lift one side of dough up over the filling and fold to enclose. Press down around each filling. Use a knife or ravioli cutter to cut the pastry into little squarish 'pillows'. Use the tines of a fork to press down the edges of the pillows to seal the pastry. (The *pastatelle* can be frozen at this stage.)

- Fill a deep saucepan or wok one-third full of oil and heat to 180°C or until a cube of bread turns golden in 15 seconds. Deep-fry the *pastatelle*, in batches, for 1½ minutes or until lightly golden all over. Remove with a slotted spoon and drain on paper towel. Immediately roll in the sugar to coat. Enjoy hot.

MAKES 70

2½ cups strong (00) flour

3 eggs

½ cup (250 ml) white wine

½ cup vegetable oil, plus extra, for (250 ml) deep-frying

plain flour, for dusting

caster sugar, for coating

Filling

1 kg dried chestnuts, soaked in water for 2 days in the refrigerator, then drained

1 cup raw caster sugar

125 g dark cooking chocolate (70% cocoa solids), finely grated

1 tablespoon cocoa powder

1 teaspoon ground cinnamon

1 tablespoon instant coffee, dissolved in 150 ml boiling water

½ cup (250 ml) freshly squeezed orange juice

½ cup (250 ml) anisette (anise liqueur)

Best Scones Ever

I received this recipe about ten years ago from a friend of mine and have since shared it with many friends and family. What I really love about it is that my young son can help me make it as it doesn't require a lot of ingredients and has only a couple of steps to it. My husband prefers larger, taller scones, but I like the medium size. The trick to getting a tall scone is the lemonade. I like to use Schweppes – I've found other brands don't produce as much rise.
— Gail Sanders, Watson, ACT

- Preheat the oven to 220°C and line a baking tray with baking paper.

- Sift the flour and salt into a large bowl and make a well in the centre.

- Pour the cream and lemonade into the well in the flour mixture and gently mix with a knife until the mixture just comes together. Turn the dough onto a lightly floured work surface and gently press into a 2–3 cm thick round.

- Using a 7 cm or 8 cm cutter lightly dusted with flour, cut the dough into rounds and place on the prepared tray. You may need to re-flour the cutter.

- Brush the tops with a little milk and bake for 12–14 minutes, depending on their size, until lightly golden on top.

- Remove from the oven and serve warm with whipped cream and jam.

MAKES 8–12 DEPENDING ON CUTTER

3 cups self-raising flour, plus extra, for dusting

pinch of table salt

1 cup thickened (whipping) cream

1 cup (250 ml) Schweppes lemonade

milk, for brushing

whipped cream and your favourite jam, to serve

Cookies that Taste Great (and Make You Look Awesome)

I started making these cookies when my eldest daughter was about two years old. I wanted a recipe that was quick and easy but still tasty. I found a recipe for a date slice but I knew no one in my house would eat that so I swapped the dates for chocolate and added a little more brown sugar and this choc chip cookie was born. After making hundreds of cookies and sharing the recipe with everyone who ate them, I decided to experiment and add Mars bars instead of chocolate and we were not disappointed. Since then I have baked the cookies with M&Ms, Fantales, Caramello Koalas, Cherry Ripe bars, and with added ginger and macadamia nuts, or with white chocolate and macadamia nuts. Every chocolate has tasted great in this cookie base! This recipe is also great baked as a slice and served warm with ice-cream for an easy yet fancy way to end a dinner with friends. It's so simple to make that the kids can help out but be warned: the cookie dough is as addictive as the cookies and you may find it disappearing before you get a chance to roll them. — Kristy Thomson, Birkdale, Qld

- Preheat the oven to 180°C and line two large baking trays with baking paper.

- Cream the butter and sugar in a bowl until light and fluffy. Beat in the egg until well incorporated.

- Sift in the flour and fold in gently.

- Gently fold in the chocolate confectionery.

- Roll the mixture into golfball-sized balls, place on the prepared trays, allowing room to spread between each, and flatten slightly.

- Bake for 12–15 minutes – less if you prefer a chewier cookie or longer if you prefer a crunchier one.

- Remove from the oven and cool on the trays for 5 minutes, then move to wire racks to cool.

MAKES 15 LARGE COOKIES

1 cup loosely packed soft brown sugar

90 g unsalted butter, softened

1 egg, at room temperature

1½ cups self-raising flour

1 cup of your favourite chocolate confectionery, chopped into small bits if large

Vanilla Slice

Vanilla slice takes me straight back in time to the school tuckshop. Back then, I didn't appreciate the time and skill that went into making these delicious treats. The trickiest part of this recipe is making sure the custard sets perfectly. My first couple of batches turned out a bit sloppy but I didn't let them go to waste – they were still delicious and I just ate them with a spoon. If your first attempt doesn't set right, don't be disheartened – it will still taste good. Keep trying until you get the ideal set. — Leila McKinnon

- Preheat the oven to 210°C and line two baking trays with baking paper.

- Place the sheets of puff pastry on the prepared trays and bake according to the packet directions until crisp and golden. Remove from the oven and set aside to cool.

- Heat the milk and vanilla seeds in a small saucepan over medium heat and bring to the boil, then remove from the heat.

- Place the cornflour and sugar in a heatproof bowl. Add the egg yolks and whisk until pale and creamy. Add one-third of the hot milk and stir to combine, then add the remaining hot milk and stir to combine.

- Return the mixture to the pan over low heat and bring to a gentle boil, then transfer to a bowl and leave to cool completely.

- Line a 25 cm x 12 cm straight-sided cake tin with enough plastic wrap so that it hangs over the sides. Trim the pastry sheets to fit the tin. Place one pastry sheet in the base of the tin, add the custard and evenly spread. Top with the remaining pastry sheet and refrigerate until the custard
is set, ideally overnight.

- Remove from the tin using the plastic wrap as handles, generously dust with icing sugar and cut into 6–8 slices.

MAKES 6–8

2 sheets puff pastry

2 cups (500 ml) milk

1 vanilla bean, halved lengthways and seeds scraped

100 g cornflour

½ cup caster sugar

4 egg yolks, at room temperature

sifted icing sugar, for dusting

ACKNOWLEDGEMENTS

I really believe *Australia's Favourite Recipes* captures a moment of life around our nation's dining tables, at our celebrations and in our family stories, and I am very grateful to the team that made it possible.

Fellow food lover and cookbook reader Stacey McLean from 22 Management planted the seed, and without Sean Anderson and Laura Mitchell it wouldn't have sprung to life. Mary Small and Ellie Smith from Pan Macmillan were not only the creative inspiration, they also did all the heavy lifting, and were an absolute pleasure to work with. I owe many thanks to my colleagues at the Nine Network who provided me with help and enthusiastic support, including Cameron Williams, Tim Gilbert, Stephanie Sgroi and Glen Caro.

Thanks to Corene Strauss and Carly Cullen at Legacy, who do such important work, and to Miriam Zariffa, Muriel McCabe and Pat Tompkins, thank you so much for your stories and your recipes. Thanks also to Sue Butler and Macquarie Dictionary Publishers.

Thank you to Chris Chen for the exceptional photography in the book, to Simon Bajada for beautiful food styling and to Michele Curtis for all her help in the kitchen.

Margaret Fulton: wow, my name is next to yours on a cookbook. I can't articulate how excited that makes me every time I look at it. Thank you for giving us your time, your expertise and your exquisite berry meringue cake recipe, and thank you for bringing an end to the bland old days.

Thanks Mum and Dad for your recipes and for giving me the gift of never being afraid of taking on any challenge, and to all my family for the meals we've shared in celebration, commiseration, and just because we love each other's company.

And thank you to my husband David for never failing to remind me of the dismal first meal I ever made for him, and for his enthusiastic appreciation of everything I've cooked since.

But most of all, thank you to all the contributors to this project. Your recipes, stories and photos are family treasures, thanks for sharing them with us all.

Leila McKinnon

INDEX

A Plum book
First published in 2012 by
Pan Macmillan Australia Pty Limited
Level 25, 1 Market Street,
Sydney, NSW 2000, Australia

Level 1, 15–19 Claremont Street,
South Yarra, Victoria 3141, Australia

A CIP catalogue record for this book is available from the National Library of Australia.

Photography by Chris Chen
Designed by Kirby Armstrong
Food preparation by Michele Curtis
Prop styling by Simon Bajada
Typeset by Pauline Haas
Edited by Belinda So
Indexed by Jo Rudd

Colour reproduction by Splitting Image, Clayton, Victoria
Printed and bound in China by 1010 Printing International Limited

The publisher would like to thank Step Back Antiques for their generosity in providing
props for the book.

10 9 8 7 6 5 4 3 2 1